D1566180

Earnings Management:
An Executive Perspective

Thomas E. McKee, Ph.D., CPA

Australia · Canada · Mexico · Singapore · Spain · United Kingdom · United States

Earnings Management: An Executive Perspective
Thomas E. McKee, Ph.D., CPA

COPYRIGHT © 2005 Texere, an imprint of Thomson/South-Western, a part of The Thomson Corporation. Thomson and the Star logo are trademarks used herein under license.

Composed by: Chip Butzko, Encouragement Press, L.L.C.

Printed in the United States of America by R.R. Donnelley, Crawfordsville

1 2 3 4 5 07 06 05

This book is printed on acid-free paper.

ISBN: 0-324-22325-0

This publication is designed to provide accurate and authoritative information in regard to the subject matter covered. It is sold with the understanding that the publisher is not engaged in rendering legal, accounting or other professional services. If expert assistance is required, the services of a competent professional person should be sought.

The names of all companies or products mentioned herein are used for identification purposes only and may be trademarks or registered trademarks of their respective owners. Texere disclaims any affiliation, association, connection with, sponsorship, or endorsements by such owners.

For permission to use material from this text or product, submit a request online at http://www.thomsonrights.com.

Library of Congress Cataloging in Publication Number is available. See page 206 for details.

For more information about our products, contact us at:

Thomson Learning Academic Resource Center
1-800-423-0563

Thomson Higher Education
5191 Natorp Boulevard
Mason, Ohio 45040
USA

Asia (including India)
Thomson Learning
5 Shenton Way
#01-01 UIC Building
Singapore 068808

Australia/New Zealand
Thomson Learning Australia
102 Dodds Street
Southbank, Victoria 3006
Australia

Canada
Thomson Nelson
1120 Birchmount Road
Toronto, Ontario
M1K 5G4
Canada

Latin America
Thomson Learning
Seneca, 53
Colonia Polanco
11560 Mexico
D.F. Mexico

UK/Europe/Middle East/Africa
Thomson Learning
High Holborn House
50/51 Bedford Row
London WC1R 4LR
United Kingdom

Spain (including Portugal)
Thomson Paraninfo
Calle Magallanes, 25
28015 Madrid, Spain

DEDICATION

This book is dedicated to the memory of my wife, Carolyn Sue Whitson McKee. Her love and support over many years helped me to achieve numerous things in life that would otherwise have been impossible. Her positive spirit, love, and influence are also visible in our children, Misty, Jennifer, and Brandon. Every day I miss her very much.

I would also like to dedicate this book to the memory of my parents, Patricia Claire Rorke Blakely and Carrick McKee. They both, each in their own distinct way, provided love and had a positive influence on my life.

A Note about the Cases

This book uses financial statements and other information from a large number of actual companies in the form of cases to demonstrate how different financial accounting treatments, options, or generally accepted accounting principle alternatives have been implemented in real life. This does not imply that these companies engaged in earnings management.

CONTENTS

ABOUT THE AUTHOR

Thomas E. McKee, Ph.D., CPA, CMA, CIA is the Blackburn Childers and Stigall Faculty Fellow in Accounting and a Professor in the Department of Accountancy at East Tennessee State University, Johnson City, Tennessee. He also holds a current part-time appointment as a Professor II at the Norwegian School of Economics and Business Administration (Norway) where he teaches yearly in the graduate auditing program.

Dr. McKee was a Fulbright lecturer and research scholar during the 1998 Fall semester at the Norwegian School of Economics and Business Administration. He was also a Visiting Professor at the College of Charleston, Charleston, South Carolina, during 2003-2004, Massey University (New Zealand) in 1991, the Norwegian School of Economics and Business Administration (Norway) during 1987-1988, and the University of Tennessee in 1980. He has also been a member of the accounting faculties at the University of Maryland and Georgia State University. Previous to that, he worked as a staff and senior accountant with Price Waterhouse.

Professor McKee has authored or co-authored more than 100 publications, including 65 journal articles and nine books or monographs. His books include *Auditing* (through 5th edition) and *Analytical Auditing* (1989). His articles have appeared in the following publications: *The European Journal of Operational Research, The Journal of Accounting, Taxation and Finance for Business, Journal of Accounting Education, Journal of Information Technology, International*

Journal of Intelligent Systems in Accounting, Finance, and Management, Journal of Forecasting, Advances in Accounting, The Accounting Historians Journal, Journal of Accountancy, Internal Auditor, and *The CPA Journal.*

Professor McKee regularly makes speeches and technical presentations on different contemporary business, accounting, and auditing topics. He has presented over 100 seminars throughout the United States for CPA firms, business organizations, and state CPA societies. He was previously selected "Outstanding Discussion Leader of the Year" by the Tennessee Society of CPAs.

Dr. McKee has also provided consulting services to businesses and CPA firms. Services have included financial planning, plant feasibility studies, business valuations, Accounting systems design, EDP control reviews, and opinion letters on various technical accounting and auditing issues. He has also acted as an expert witness in a variety of litigation cases.

PREFACE

The job of executives could easily be defined as *the creation and management of earnings*. Executives make numerous decisions affecting earnings every day. That means that every executive is engaged, either passively or actively, in earnings management.

Those executives who are not familiar with the concepts described in this book make earnings management decisions by default. Their passive earnings management may or may not be fully beneficial to the company. The executives who have a comprehensive knowledge of earnings management are able to make active, informed financial decisions that are highly beneficial to the company that employs them.

Executives have the responsibility to see that the financial picture portrayed for their business presents the business in the best light possible so that it will have access to capital and other resources at the lowest possible cost. This means that every executive needs to be able to understand the earnings impact of each of their accounting and operating decisions. The choices they make are commonly called "earnings management," which is defined in this book as:

> *". . . reasonable and* legal *management decision making and reporting intended to achieve and disclose stable and predictable financial results."*

Unfortunately, over the years a few individuals have felt pressure to go to extremes in manipulating financial statements, to the extent even of committing fraud. The activities that go beyond responsible earnings management can be called "cooking the books," which may be defined as illegal activities designed to report financial results that do not conform to economic reality.

The vast majority of executives do not need to resort to cooking the books; they can find plenty of room within the rules of generally accepted accounting principles to help them reach desired earnings goals. This is possible because either accounting rules are very non-specific or they permit a number of acceptable alternative treatments. In fact, the financial press often severely criticizes the looseness of accounting rules for allowing executives excessive latitude in reporting results. The chairman of the leading accounting rule making body has even stated:

> *"There's virtually no standard that the FASB has ever written that is free from judgment in its application."*[1]

To manage earnings, executives do not have to be expert accountants. There are a small number of basic principles and approaches that can easily help achieve desired financial results. In fact failure to understand and properly apply these principles, as explained in this book, means that a company's financial results may be unnecessarily chaotic, penalizing shareholders through decreased stock prices.

The objective of this book is to demystify earnings management by carefully illustrating thirty or so common methods to achieve desired financial reporting results legally. Each chapter provides underlying concepts, accounting requirements, and illustrative examples. Numerous recent actual company cases from some of America's best known companies illustrate how financial statements may be affected by the choice of accounting alternatives. All are legal.

Executives reading this book will gain valuable knowledge about earnings management concepts and techniques. Other readers, such as investors who want to better understand reported earnings, will gain greater insight into the management decisions that can shape financial statements and the underlying quality of earnings. Students will also benefit from this book because it explains a great deal about finance and accounting using simple language in a practical context. The numerous cases reveal how well-managed companies make a wide variety of accounting choices.

---

[1] Beresford, D. R., Chairman (1987-97) of the Financial Accounting Standards Board, quoted by F. Norris, "From the Chief Accountant, a Farewell Ledger." *New York Times,* June 1, 1997.

1 WHAT IS EARNINGS MANAGEMENT?

This chapter defines earnings management and explains the difference between legal *and* illegal *earnings management (commonly called "cooking the books").*

Earnings, sometimes called the "bottom line" or "net income," are the single most important item in financial statements. They indicate the extent to which a company has engaged in value-added activities. They are a signal that helps direct resource allocation in capital markets. In fact, the theoretical value of a company's stock is the present value of its future earnings. Increased earnings represent an increase in company value, while decreased earnings signal a decrease in that value.[1]

Given the importance of earnings, it is no surprise that company management has a vital interest in how they are reported. That is why every executive needs to understand the effect of their accounting choices so they can make the best possible decisions for the company. They must, in other words, learn to manage earnings.

Earnings management may be defined as "reasonable and legal management decision making and reporting intended to achieve stable and predictable financial results." Earnings management is not to be confused with illegal activities to manipulate financial statements and report results that do not reflect economic reality. These types of activities, popularly known as "cooking the books," involve misrepresenting financial results.

Many executives face a lot of pressure to cross the line from earnings management to cooking the books. A 1998 survey at a conference sponsored by *CFO*

---

[1]Lev, B. "On the Usefulness of Earnings and Earnings Research: Lessons and Directions From Two Decades of Empirical Research." *Journal of Accounting Research*, 27 Supplement (1989): 153-201.

Magazine found that 78 percent of the chief financial officers (CFOs) in attendance had been asked to cast financial results in a better light, though still using generally accepted accounting principles (GAAP). Half of them complied with the request. Worse, however, 45 percent of the group attendees reported that they had been asked to *misrepresent* their company's financial results—and 38 percent admit with complying.

The intense pressure to report better earnings was confirmed by a similar survey at a *Business Week* CFO conference. It found that 55 percent of the CFOs had been asked to misrepresent financial results, and 17 percent had complied.[2]

HOW WIDESPREAD IS EARNINGS MANAGEMENT?

Research on earnings management "suggests that *this is a pervasive phenomenon:* We estimate that 8-12 percent of firms with small pre-managed earnings decreases manipulate earnings to achieve earnings increases, and 30-44 percent of the firms with small pre-managed losses manage earnings to create positive earnings (emphasis added)."[3] In other words, a large number of companies are using earnings management either to maintain steady earnings growth or to avoid reporting red ink.

One study estimates that operating profits for the Standard & Poor's 500 stocks "have been inflated by at least 10 percent per year for the past two decades, thanks to a mix of one-time write-offs and other accounting tricks."[4] Since it is widely accepted that operating profits are highly correlated to stock prices over the long term, this means that the prices of S&P 500 stocks, some of the best companies in the world, have consistently been enhanced by earnings management techniques. The practice is indeed pervasive.

General Electric (GE) was one of America's best-loved stocks as it achieved $10.7 billion in earnings for fiscal year 2000. It had had a 482 percent total return over the previous five-year period. GE's chief executive, Jack Welch, was considered a management genius. He disputed the idea that the company managed earnings even using legal methods.

The facts show that GE had, through fiscal year 2000, had 100 consecutive quarters of increased earnings from continuing operations. This even surpassed Wal-Mart's 99-quarter streak that ended in 1996.[5] The streak is one of the reasons that in 2001 GE had the stock market's biggest capitalization, $590 billion.

---

[2] Earnings Management, p. 1. *http:/www.romeassoc.com/inv_lit/archives/earnings.htm.* Accessed June 12, 2001.

[3] Burgstahler, D., and I. Dichev. "Earnings Management to Avoid Earnings Decreases and Losses." *Journal of Accounting and Economics,* 24 (1997): 101.

[4] "Economic Focus: Taking the Measure." *The Economist,* November 24, 2001, p. 72.

[5] Birger, Jon. "GE's Glowing Numbers." Money.com. *http://www.money.com/money/depts/investing/ge.* Accessed June 12, 2001.

GE's earnings were so predictable they were almost a straight upward line. In the calendar year 2000, *The Value Line Investment Survey* gave GE its highest score of 100 for earnings predictability.[6]

How did GE do it? One undeniable explanation is the fundamental growth of its eight industrial businesses and 24 financial-services units. "We're the best company in the world," Dennis Dammerman, GE's chief financial officer, declared.

But another explanation is earnings management, the orchestrated timing of gains and losses to smooth out bumps and especially avoid a decline. Among big companies, GE has long been known as "a relatively aggressive practitioner of earnings management," to quote Martin Sankey, a CS First Boston Inc. analyst.[7]

Many people believe that this type of long-run earnings increase just does not happen by chance. Reporter Jon Birger has said, "GE has employed a number of confusing but apparently legal gimmicks to achieve its vaunted consistency. No company, not even one as well managed as GE, has 100 quarters of uninterrupted growth without resorting to some fancy accounting—or, as the mannered folks on Wall Street like to call it, earnings management."[8]

BY ANY OTHER NAME

A number of phrases have been used to describe earnings management activities:

- Income smoothing
- Accounting hocus-pocus
- Financial statement management
- The numbers game
- Aggressive accounting
- Reengineering the income statement
- Juggling the books
- Creative accounting
- Financial statement manipulation
- Accounting magic
- Borrowing income from the future
- Banking income for the future
- Financial shenanigans
- Window dressing
- Accounting alchemy

---

[6]*The Value Line Investment Survey.* "Ratings and Reports." New York: Value Line Publishing Inc., April 14, 2000, p. 1011.

[7]Smith, R., S. Lipin, and A. K. Naj. "Managing Profits: How General Electric Damps Fluctuations In Its Annual Earnings." *Wall Street Journal,* November 3, 1994.

[8]Birger, "GE's Glowing Numbers," above, n. 5.

There is no standard, universally accepted definition for any of these terms. People use them in different ways and with different degrees of appreciation to cover a wide variety of activities, many perfectly legal. This tends to blur the distinction between entirely legal earnings management and illegally cooking the books.

ACHIEVING EARNINGS MANAGEMENT

The definition of earnings management that we are using describes reasonable and proper practices that are part of a well-managed business that delivers value to shareholders. Earnings management is primarily achieved by management actions that make it easier to achieve desired earnings levels through:

- Accounting choices from among GAAP.
- Operating decisions (sometimes called *economic earnings management).*

An example of a GAAP *accounting choice* would be whether a company should (a) be a voluntary early adopter of a new accounting standard or (b) wait two years until adoption of the new accounting standard is required of all companies.

A choice of this type occurred when the Financial Accounting Standards Board (FASB) issued a new standard for pensions (FAS No. 87) effective in 1987. Firms could choose to adopt the new standard as early as 1985. The new standard permitted companies whose pension assets exceeded their pension liabilities to count the difference as income. Not surprisingly, "Almost all of the firms that opted for an early adoption boosted their earnings by it."[9]

An example of a proper management *operating decision* would be whether or not to implement a special discount or incentive program to increase sales near the end of a quarter when revenue targets are not being met. Other examples of operating decisions would be whether to invest in new equipment or hire additional employees. Companies have to make these types of decisions constantly. Earnings management via operating decisions is sometimes called "economic earnings management" because it attempts to manage the cash flows and thus the revenues and expenses associated with operations.

There are real economic costs to this type of earnings management. For example, if you eliminate normal maintenance procedures in one period to reduce maintenance costs, you are likely to incur higher operating costs caused by the lack of maintenance in either the next or some future period. Earnings management via accounting choices similarly may result in real economic costs. For example, a company may have to pay a higher bonus in a subsequent period due to accounting earnings management.[10] Figure 1.1 illustrates how management may manage reported earnings through either operating decisions or accounting choices:

---

[9]Lev, "On the Usefulness of Earnings," above, n. 1.
[10]Ziv, A. "Discussion of 'Earnings Management and the Revelation Principle'." *Review of Accounting Studies, 3, (1998): 35-40.*

Figure 1.1. Effects of Operating versus Accounting Choices

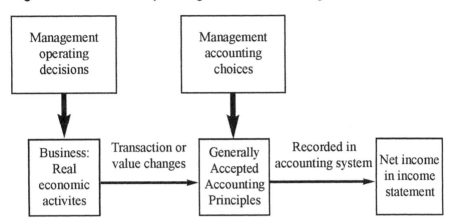

This book will focus on explaining earnings management via accounting choices. Earnings management though operating decisions is not discussed because it can vary so widely from industry to industry and business to business.

BENEFITS TO SHAREHOLDERS

A common criticism of earnings management is that it reduces transparency by obscuring the "true" earnings of the company. However, leading academics argue that both the level and patterns of earnings convey information and that even when earnings management conceals information, it can still be beneficial to shareholders. Arya, Glover, and Sunder state:

> *"That earnings management reduces transparency is a simplistic idea. A fundamental feature of decentralized organizations is the dispersal of information across people. Different people know different things and nobody knows everything. In such an environment, a managed earnings stream can convey more information than an unmanaged earnings stream. A smooth car ride is not only comfortable, but it also reassures the passenger about the driver's expertise."* [11]

SELECTIVE MISREPRESENTATION HYPOTHESIS

There is no doubt that the GAAP reporting rules are often arbitrary, complicated, and, occasionally potentially misleading. Some highly respected academic researchers believe this is no accident, characterizing the principles as means to

---

[11]Arya, A., J. C. Glover, and S. Sunder. "Are Unmanaged Earnings Always Better For Shareholders?" *Accounting Horizons*, supplement 2003, p. 111-112.

selective financial misrepresentation. Management, shareholders, auditors, and standard setters are motivated to support GAAP, they suggest, because selective misrepresentation of economic reality benefits them in some way.

"Corporate America often wants exceptions to broad accounting principles," *Business Week* has said. Consider Financial Accounting Standard 133, which dictates accounting for derivatives and hedging. To avoid "unpredictable swings in corporate earnings" the FASB "carved out exceptions for hedging deals, forward contracts or materials, insurance policies, and other special cases." "The result: FAS 133 and its supporting documents weigh in at 800 pages—and it's still a work in progress."[12]

As long ago as 1984, in a *Business Week* article titled "The SEC Turns up the Heat on 'Cooked Books,'" one of the commissioners of the Securities and Exchange Commission was quoted as saying that the SEC was also concentrating enforcement on "'cute accounting,' the stretching and bending, rather than out-and-out breaking, of accounting rules."[13] Two decades later the SEC is still dealing with the same issues even though it has the legal power to set and enforce, with civil and criminal penalties, both accounting and auditing standards. In 2003, *Business Week* said the SEC was "writing or implementing standards that could force companies to recast their results and disclose much more information. It's the biggest advance in public company accounting since the securities laws of the 1930s."[14] The two-decade delay suggests that even the SEC has had, and may still have, some motivation to support GAAP that allow a variety of representations of economic reality.

Professor Lawrence Revsine comments on this hypothesis:

> *"To summarize, research evidence is consistent with the notion that managers use latitude in existing financial reporting to benefit themselves. In several of these studies, this behavior simultaneously benefits shareholders. This reinforces the point that misrepresentation conveys potentially widespread benefits. Indeed, this characteristic of "shared benefits" may be crucial to the survival of selective misrepresentation."*[15]

I do not believe that the word "misrepresentation" is appropriate to describe legal earnings management. It implies that managers know what "true" earnings are and are deliberately trying to show a different amount. In many cases managers are simply making choices that increase earnings because accounting standards permit them to do so.

---

[12]"FASB: Rewriting the Book on Bookkeeping." *Business Week* Online, May 20, 2002. *http://www.businessweek.com/magazine/content/02_20/b3782094. him.*
[13]"The SEC Turns Up The Heat on 'Cooked Books.'" *Business Week*, September 3, 1984, pp. 63-64.
[14]"Cleaning Up The Numbers." *Business Week Online*, March 24, 2003. *http://www.businessweek.com/bw50/content/mar2003/a3826040.htm.*
[15]Revsine, L. "The Selective Financial Misrepresentation Hypothesis." *Accounting Horizons,* December 1991, pp. 16-27.

In fact, many people believe that only GAAP defines what "earnings" or "income" actually is. Thus, if management is following GAAP, earnings are not being misrepresented. Critics to this argument, however, point out that the standard setters who write the GAAP rules must have some theoretical concept of "true" earnings or income that they are attempting to measure via the GAAP rules. I believe that true earnings exist only as a theoretical concept and do not necessarily describe an amount that is not known or knowable by management. This conclusion is supported by arguments made by a current member of the FASB, which establishes GAAP, and her co-author who write:

> *"Earnings can be defined using the economics-based definition of earnings developed by J. Hicks in his 1939 book Value and Capital. 'Hicksian' income corresponds to the amount that can be consumed (that is paid out in dividends) during a period, while leaving the firm equally well off at the beginning and end of the period . . . We define earnings quality as the extent to which reported earnings faithfully represent Hicksian income . . . The construct (Hicksian income) thus allows us to consider what reported earnings would look like in the absence of reporting rules and their implementation . . . Because Hicksian income is not observable, it is not possible to quantify the differences . . . between the Hicksian earnings concept and reported earning generated by U.S. GAAP, along with preparers' implementation decisions. "*[16]

This previous discussion supports the argument that "true" earnings are not observable and, therefore, not a reasonable standard against which to judge managements earnings decisions.

It is clear from the research that:

- GAAP permits many accounting choices and requires many estimations, thereby facilitating earnings management.
- Because all companies make innumerable operating and accounting choices, they must engage in some form of earnings management even if this is by default rather than active choice.
- Many parties benefit from active earnings management.

Since earnings management must be practiced, whether by active choice or by default, smart executives will learn to use the techniques discussed in this book whenever they seem appropriate.

ACCOUNTING EARNINGS MANAGEMENT

Earnings management activities may occur (1) because managers have flexibility in making accounting or operating choices or (2) because managers are trying to

---

[16]Schipper, K., and L. Vincent. "Earnings Quality." *Accounting Horizons*, supplement, 2003, pp. 97-98.

convey private information to financial statement users. It is important for readers of financial statements to determine which type is being practiced and to understand its significance. Some examples:

- *Flexible accounting or operating choices.* Managers may adopt a depreciable life for a new computer chip plant that is at the high end of industry norms in order to lower depreciation expense and thus maximize reported earnings for future periods. The aim here is to manage earnings (and thus share prices) in a direction desired by current shareholders.

- *Private information.* Managers may adopt a depreciable life for a new computer chip plant that is substantially less than industry norms because anticipated technological changes make it likely that the plant will be obsolete sooner than has been the norm for the industry. The motive here is to give stakeholders information not otherwise available so they can adjust their expectations appropriately.

  Careful release of such information may lower earnings and the share price for the company, but if the information conveys significant new news to analysts and other users of financial statements, they may also adjust earnings estimates (and share prices) downward for other companies in the industry, so that the company revealing the information may actually feel some positive impact on its share prices because it is perceived as having a higher "quality of earnings." This concept is discussed in more detail later.

ACCOUNTING CHOICES

Accounting choices should be made within the framework of generally accepted accounting principles. GAAP is the set of rules, practices, and conventions that describe what is acceptable financial reporting for external stakeholders. The main source of GAAP for public companies are the Financial Accounting Statements (FAS) of the FASB, although there are also several other sources.

Some people find it quite surprising that a single, normal, everyday accounting choice may be either legal or illegal. The difference between a legal and an illegal accounting choice is often merely the degree to which the choice is carried out. To better understand this, think about driving a ear. Driving is inherently neither legal nor illegal. Much depends on the law in the jurisdiction in which you are driving. If the speed limit is 65 mph, for instance, and your speed is 60 mph, your driving is within the legal limits. On the other hand, if your speed is 100 mph, you are clearly driving illegally.

The problem with many accounting choices is that there is no clear posted limit beyond which a choice is obviously illegal. Thus, a perfectly routine accounting decision, such as expense estimation, may be illegal if the estimated amount is extreme but perfectly legal if it is reasonable. GAAP does not tell managers what specifically is normal and what is extreme. It is more like a speed limit sign that just says "Don't Drive Too Fast!"

Product warranty cost estimation is an example of an accounting decision many managers have to make. GAAP normally requires that this estimate be recorded as an expense in the same fiscal year as the revenue from the product is recorded: If you sell a hair dryer for $30 and offer a free refund or replacement if it breaks within one year from date of purchase, you should estimate this warranty cost and record it as an expense in the same fiscal year as the $30 revenue from the hair dryer. This follows a basic accounting concept of matching expenses with related revenue. If you assume that warranty cost averages $2.75 per unit sold, the items on the income statement would look something like this:

Revenue	$30.00
Less: Warranty expense	2.75
Income	$27.25

However, the fact that warranty costs will be $2.75 per unit is not always so clear. Assume that for the past five years, average unit warranty costs for the hair dryer have ranged from $2.50 to $2.80, with no specific pattern being apparent. A financial manager who wanted to report the highest possible current period income would be justified in using $2.50 per unit for the current year's expense estimate even though $2.50 is the bottom of the historical range. That same manager might even be justified in using $2.25 per unit if there was evidence that improved quality control during the current fiscal year would lower future warranty costs. But what if that manager used $1.25 per unit simply because that figure for warranty expense would make it possible to achieve a desired net income target for the fiscal year? Since the $1.25 has no reasonable support, using it would be crossing the line to financial fraud—even though GAAP does not draw that clear a line.

THE FRAUD ISSUE

Financial fraud has been defined by the National Association of Certified Fraud Examiners as "the intentional, deliberate misstatement or omission of material facts, or accounting data, which is misleading and, when considered with all the information made available, would cause the reader to change or alter his or her judgment or decision."[17]

Earnings management is at the legal end of a continuum. Financial fraud is at the illegal end. Fraud clearly violates GAAP, since the FASB has said, "Accrual accounting uses accrual, deferral, and allocation procedures whose goal is to relate revenue, expenses, gains, and losses to periods *to respect an entity's performance*

---

[17]National Association of Certified Fraud Examiners, Cooking the Books: *What Every Accountant Should Know About Fraud.* Self-Study Workbook, No. 92-5401. Austin, TX: NACFE, 1993, p. 12.

during a period." (emphasis added)[18] The key concept in this definition is that GAAP-based accounting is supposed to reflect, not distort or obscure, true economic performance. GAAP may also be violated by actions that do not sink to fraud, such as "overly aggressive accounting," because that may distort or obscure the true economic performance of a business.

Using data from our previous warranty expense estimation example, Figure 1.2 illustrates the concept of a reported earnings continuum from merely conservative to fraudulent. Figure 1.2 assumes there was evidence that quality control improvements could lower warranty costs to $2.25.

Figure 1.2. The Earnings Management—Fraud Continuum[19]

Conservative Accounting	Neutral Accounting		Aggressive Accounting	Fraudulent Accounting
$2.80	$2.65	$2.50	$2.25	$1.25
Within GAAP				*Violates GAAP*

As our assumptions change, the interpretation changes. Assume there was absolutely no evidence, merely management optimism, that quality control changes during the year would lower future warranty costs under the historical $2.50 to $2.80 range. Now management has no real support for estimating that product warranty costs will be $2.25 per unit. The $2.25 figure should now be considered overly aggressive and beyond the bounds of GAAP. This scenario is illustrated in Figure 1.3.

Figure 1.3. Overly Aggressive Earnings on the Continuum[20]

Conservative Accounting	Neutral Accounting	Aggressive Accounting	Overly Aggressive Accounting	Fraudulent Accounting
$2.80	$2.65	$2.50	$2.25	$1.25
Within GAAP				*Violates GAAP*

---

[18]Financial Accounting Standards Board (FASB). 1985. *Statement of Financial Accounting Concepts,* No. 6, paragraph 145.

[19]Dechow, P. M., and D. J. Skinner, "Earnings Management: Reconciling the Views of Accounting Academics, Practitioners, and Regulators." *Accounting Horizons,* 14, No. 2, adapted from page 239.

[20]Dechow, R M., and D. J. Skinner. "Earnings Management: Reconciling The Views of Accounting Academics, Practitioners, and Regulators." *Accounting Horizons,* Vol. 14, No. 2, adapted from page 239.

It is clear from the two figures that there is no "bright line" in GAAP to tell managers what is and what is not acceptable. Management is simply expected to make choices that appropriately reflect a company's economic performance. What is appropriate for one company may not be appropriate for another.

THE HEALTHSOUTH EXAMPLE

Richard M. Scrushy, CEO of HealthSouth Corporation, started the company with $1 million in seed capital and turned into a multibillion-dollar hospital chain. In the decade after HealthSouth Corporation went public in 1986 it posted annual double-digit profit increases. The stock price soared an average of 31 percent *per year* between 1987 and 1997.

Things started to get more difficult in 1997 when Congress slashed Medicare reimbursements to hospitals and when expected economies of scale for large hospital chains proved difficult to realize. Management tried to improve operating efficiency and cut costs, and the financial reports made it appear that they had succeeded in these efforts. It later appeared that the reported earnings were not accurate.[21]

> *"Although sales rose only 3 percent in 1999 and 2000, operating earnings soared an incredible 143 percent. Now investigators say that these fantastic numbers were just that—fantasy. Fraud, not efficiency and cost-cutting, accounted for the huge discrepancy between sales and profits.*
>
> *Securities & Exchange Commission and Justice Department investigators have accused Scrushy, 50, of cooking his books to inflate profits by at least $1.4 billion since 1999. The government complaint describes the most brazen sort of fraud: a group of people gathering in a room and simply making up numbers. Scrushy has denied the charges, but several of his former lieutenants, such as former Chief Financial Officer William T. Owens, have pleaded guilty and are cooperating with the investigation. Scrushy, founder and CEO, was fired on March 31."* [22]

INTENT TO DECEIVE

A key element in financial fraud is intent to deceive. This poses a difficult question in many possible fraud situations because managerial intent with respect to accounting choices is unobservable and often can only be inferred from management actions.

Fraud is usually carried out for personal gain. The gain may be direct, such as a higher bonus for the year, or it could be indirect, such as job security or maintaining a career path as a "high flyer."

---

[21]Haddad, C., A. Weintraub, and B. Grow. "Too Good to Be True: Why HealthSouth CEO Scrushy Began Deep-Frying the Chain's Books." Business Week Online, April 14, 2003, http://www.businessweek.com/magazine/content/03_15/b3828078_mzO56.htm.
[22]Ibid.

A wide variety of state and federal laws deal with fraud. Violators may find themselves subject to both civil (monetary damages) and criminal (jail time) penalties and may be prosecuted under more than one of these laws. Among the most stringent of these laws are the federal securities statutes starting with the 1933 and 1934 Securities and Exchange Commission Acts. These give considerable power over the financial markets and financial reporting to the SEC. That is partly why the SEC is a key player in promoting GAAP, making their use mandatory for the annual reports and financial statements of the 14,000 or so U.S. public companies.

Managers whose financial statements reflect any of the following activities may be committing fraud even if they do not think of their actions as fraud:

- Recording fictitious sales.
- Recording sales when there is a right of return and return is expected.
- Recording sales when shipping unfinished products.
- Backdating sales invoices.
- Failing to properly record expenses.
- Engaging in barter transactions where the goods or services exchanged are substantially overvalued or undervalued.
- Overvaluing assets.
- Improperly capitalizing expenses.

THE SARBANES-OXLEY ACT OF 2002

The actual incidence of reported and detected fraud in the United States is relatively low. T. J. F. Bishop notes that, in 1999, the *Wall Street Journal* reported only 25 new cases of alleged material fraud in financial statements. During the same period, 8,873 audits of public companies were reported. That would constitute an annual fraud rate of 0.3 percent for public companies—relatively low compared to the failure rate in other professions.[23] However, this statistic addresses only the frequency of frauds and not their size or economic impact.

A number of spectacularly large business failures, including Enron and WorldCom, involved either suspicions or allegations of fraud. These failures created negative publicity and loss of confidence in the capital markets. The U.S. Congress responded to the apparent public outrage by passing the Sarbanes-Oxley Act of 2002 (SOA) to remedy perceived deficiencies in financial reporting. All financial executives should be familiar with the main provisions of this law. (These provisions are discussed in Chapter 5.)

---

[23]Bishop, T. J. F. "Auditing for Fraud: Implications of Current Market Trends and Potential Responses." *The Auditor's Report, 24 (2001):* 13-15.

2 POPULAR EARNINGS MANAGEMENT TECHNIQUES

This chapter briefly surveys a wide variety of popular legal earnings management techniques discussed in detail in later chapters.

The most successful and widely used earnings management techniques can be classified into twelve categories. This chapter briefly overviews and lists some of the most common techniques within each category. More detail on these techniques, including the underlying concepts, GAAP requirements, illustrative numeric examples, and actual company cases containing accounting applications are to be found in later chapters.

"COOKIE JAR RESERVE" TECHNIQUES

A normal feature of GAAP-based accrual accounting is that management must estimate and record obligations that will paid in the future as a result of events or transactions in the current fiscal year. Since the future events cannot be known with certainty at the time of estimation, there is often substantial uncertainty surrounding the estimation process. In other words, there is no *right* answer. There is only a range of reasonably possible answers. From this range, GAAP insists that management select a single estimate. The selection process provides an opportunity for earnings management.

When management selects an estimation from the high end of the range of reasonably possible expenses, the effect is to record more expense in the current fiscal period than would be recorded if a lower estimate had been selected. Recording more expense in the current fiscal period may make it possible to record less in a future fiscal period. Thus management creates a "cookie jar reserve" [also called "financial slack"] that they can tap into later to get an earnings boost.

Of course, if in the future expenses actually turn out to be at the high end of the estimation range, the cookie jar will be empty. There will then be no earnings boost. However, if future expenses actually turn out to be in the middle or low end of the estimation range, the over accrual from the previous period may be taken into earnings.

Common areas where cookie jar reserves are created are in:

- Estimating sales returns and allowances.
- Estimating bad debt write-offs.
- Estimating inventory write-downs.
- Estimating warranty costs.
- Estimating pension expenses.
- Terminating pension plans.
- Estimating percentage of completion for long-term contracts.

"BIG BATH" TECHNIQUES

A somewhat rare occurrence for many companies is when, to remain competitive, they must substantially restructure or eliminate operations or subsidiaries. When this happens, GAAP permits management to record an estimated charge against earnings [a loss] for the cost of implementing the change. This estimated loss is usually reported as a nonrecurring charge against income, which means that it is not reported in regular operating earnings.

Charging a large loss against current earnings typically has a negative impact on the current stock price because it is associated with bad news about the company's competitiveness. However, if the charge and related operational changes are viewed as positive, the stock price may strongly rebound very quickly.

"Big bath" techniques are used in the belief that if you must report bad news, i.e., a loss from substantial restructuring, it is better to report it all at once and get it out of the way. Accordingly, since many such charges are based on estimates, it is better to estimate losses on the high side to avoid possible earnings surprises later, as would happen if you selected middle or low-side estimates only to find out in a later period that the expenses had come in on the high side.

Common circumstances where the big bath approach may be applied are in:

- Operations restructuring.
- Troubled debt restructuring.
- Asset impairment and write-down.
- Operations disposal.

"BIG BET ON THE FUTURE" TECHNIQUES

A company that acquires another company may be said to have made a "big bet on the future." This bet may even be a sure thing in terms of increasing reported earnings of the acquiring company if the acquisition is properly planned. Current GAAP requires that acquisitions be recorded under the "Purchase" method of accounting. Big bet techniques include:

- *Writing off in-process research and development costs for the company acquired.* This technique allows a substantial portion of the purchase price to be written off against current earnings in the acquisition year, protecting future earnings from these charges. This means that future earnings will be higher than they would have been otherwise.
- *Integrating the earnings of the acquired company into corporate consolidated earnings.* Current earnings of an acquired company may be consolidated with parent company earnings—providing an automatic earnings boost if the subsidiary was purchased on favorable terms.

The big bet techniques basically permit a company to buy a guaranteed boost in current or future earnings by acquiring another company.

"FLUSHING" THE INVESTMENT PORTFOLIO

Companies often buy stock in other companies either to invest excess funds or to achieve some type of strategic alliance. GAAP presumes that investments of less than 20 percent of the stock of another company are passive investments and therefore the investing company need not include a share of the investee's net income in its financial statements, as it must do for higher ownership percentages. There are detailed rules on how to report passive investments.

GAAP requires that these investments be classified into one of two portfolio categories, each with a different accounting treatment:

1. *"Trading" securities.* Any changes in the market value of these securities during a fiscal period, or actual gains or losses from sales, are reported in operating income.
2. *"Available-for-sale" securities.* Any change in market value during a fiscal period is reported in "other comprehensive income components" at the bottom of the income statement, *not* in operating income. When these securities are sold, however, any gain or loss is reported in operating income.

The GAAP requirements for investments offer an opportunity for earnings management through the following techniques:

- *Timing sales of securities that have gained value.* When additional earnings are needed, sell a portfolio security that has an unrealized gain. The gain will be reported in operating earnings.
- *Timing sales of securities that have lost value.* When it seems useful to report lower earnings, sell a security that has an unrealized loss. The loss will be reported in operating earnings.

- *Change of holding intent.* Management can decide to change its intent with respect to a security and reclassify it from the trading security portfolio to the available-for-sale portfolio, or vice versa. This would have the effect of moving any unrealized gain or loss on the security to or from the income statement.
- *Write-down of "impaired" securities.* Securities that have an apparent long-term decline in fair market value can be written down to the reduced value regardless of their portfolio classification.

Bonds that are bought to generate short-run trading gains are also classified as "trading" securities and are treated the same as stock investments in the "trading" category. Bond investments held for the longer term are classified in a different portfolio category called "held to maturity."

"THROW OUT" A PROBLEM CHILD

When earnings are dragged down by an underperforming subsidiary, and the drag is projected to increase in future periods, the "problem child" subsidiary may be "thrown out" to get rid of the drag through one of the following techniques involving accounting entity changes:

- *Sell the subsidiary.* When a subsidiary is sold, a gain or loss is reported in the current period income statement. If reporting a large loss on sale is undesirable, a spin-off should be considered.
- *Create a special-purpose entity (SPE) for financial assets.* One highly technical alternative available under GAAP is to transfer financial assets to a qualifying SPE. Such assets are deemed to have been sold and are removed from the balance sheet, with the transferor recording a gain or loss on the sale of the assets. A qualifying SPE is not consolidated with the transferor's financial statements. New accounting standards now call these entities "variable interest entities," VIE's.
- *Spin off the subsidiary.* In a spin-off, shares in the subsidiary are distributed to or exchanged with current shareholders, thus making them, not the company, owners of the problem child. No gain or loss is normally reported on a spin-off, and the negative effects of the subsidiary are removed from all financial statements because GAAP requires that prior period financial statements be restated to reflect only the results of the remaining company.
- *Exchange the stock in an "equity" method subsidiary.* It is possible to "swap" the stock in an equity method subsidiary without having any recordable gain or loss. This technique is discussed later in this chapter under Sale/Leaseback and Asset Exchange Techniques.

CHANGE GAAP

Once a company chooses the accounting principles it will use, they are rarely changed. Companies that do change have to take care that the stock market does not view the change as lowering the quality of earnings, because that may undermine the stock price. However, under the following circumstances accounting principles can be changed without affecting the stock price negatively:

- *Volunteering for a new accounting standard.* Periodically the FASB adopts new accounting standards, and usually there is an adoption window of two to three years during which the companies can adopt the standard at any time. Voluntary early adoption can provide an opportunity to manage earnings.
- *Improved revenue recognition rules.* Many industries have several alternative revenue recognition rules. Some of these are perceived as reflecting economic reality better. Timely adoption of a "better" revenue recognition rule provides an opportunity to manage earnings.
- *Improved expense recognition rule.* For companies that record certain expenses on a cash basis, a timely change to an accrual-based rule can provide an opportunity to manage earnings. Such a change may coincide with a change in corporate policies concerning the item. For example, if a company primarily compensated its executives with cash, recording these expenses when paid, a change to a deferred compensation plan could provide an opportunity to record the expense on an accrual basis and lower earnings in the year of adoption.

  Another possibility is to simply change an expense recognition rule because the new rule better matches expenses with related revenues. For example, a company might be using accelerated depreciation but decide to switch to a straight-line method because it believes straight-line depreciation better reflects the annual cost of using the asset. Straight-line depreciation results in lower initial charges, so the effect of this change would be to boost net income.

AMORTIZATION, DEPRECIATION, AND DEPLETION

The cost of long-term operating assets used or consumed is normally written off as an expense over the periods expected to be benefited. It can be expensed in three ways:

1. Amortization expense, for intangible assets such as goodwill, patents, copyrights, and trademarks.
2. Depreciation expense, for tangible assets such as buildings, machinery, and equipment.

3. Depletion expense, for natural resources that are being harvested or extracted, such as timber, coal, oil, natural gas.

Writing off long-term assets requires a variety of judgments, many of which offer an opportunity to manage earnings:

- *Selecting the write-off method.* Management has to decide what method to use to write-off newly acquired long-term operating assets. Some methods result in greater expense in the current period than others.
- *Selecting the write-off period.* Management must often estimate the "useful" life of a long-term asset, which can be substantially shorter than its actual physical life.
- *Estimating salvage value.* Some long-term assets retain substantial value at the end of their estimated useful lives. This value must be estimated in order to record the correct annual expense amount. The value may be realized 10, 15, or even 30 years in the future, so there can be a range of reasonable estimates.
- *Change to nonoperating use.* If a long-term asset is changed from operating to nonoperating use, it will no longer be necessary to record depreciation or amortization expense. This is permissible when a company ceases to use an asset for operating purposes.

SALE/LEASEBACK AND ASSET EXCHANGE TECHNIQUES

Timely disposition of long-term productive assets carried at historical cost in the balance sheet can result in the recording of unrealized gains or losses. Two methods to accomplish this are:

1. *Outright sale.* A company can sell a long-term asset that has unrealized gains or losses in a year when the sale will best enhance the financial statement. For example, suppose a building the corporation owns is carried in the balance sheet at $30 million but is really worth $50 million. If the building is sold, the $20 million gain will boost current period earnings. (Of course, this does not take into account the operational and tax considerations.)

2. *Sale/Leaseback.* It is not unusual for one company to sell an asset to another and immediately lease it back. GAAP has detailed rules about whether a lease qualifies as a *capital lease* (equivalent to retaining ownership) or an *operating lease* (equivalent to merely renting the property). Losses occurring in a sale/leaseback transaction are recognized immediately on the seller's books. Gains, however, are amortized into income, over the life of the asset if it is a capital lease or in proportion to the rental payments if it is an operating lease.

A sale/leaseback transaction offers an opportunity for managing earnings by recording the gains or losses. It also offers the opportunity to manage earnings by transforming a nondepreciable asset like land into a lease expense deduction. For example, suppose a company is recording $2 million per year of depreciation on a building it owns. Even though the land under the building is worth $100 million, GAAP allows no deduction for the use of land. If the building and land were subject to a sale/leaseback transaction which was an operating lease, the lease payments would be higher than the depreciation expense had been because the lessor, the new owner, would have to recover the cost of the land as well as the building. An annual lease payment of $5 million would thus reflect the value of both the building and the land. The $5 million lease payment would be recorded as an annual expense, providing the opportunity to lower net income by an additional $3 million beyond the previous $2 million annual depreciation deduction.

It is also possible to dispose of long-term productive assets *without* recording any gain or loss. This can be done by:

- *Exchange of similar productive assets.* Paragraph 21(b) of Accounting Principle Board Opinion (APB) 29 allows an exception to the general rule of recording a gain or loss on disposal of long-term assets when similar productive assets are exchanged. For example, Company A has a $10 million refinery in one part of the country that it swaps with Company B for a refinery of similar capacity in another part of the country so as to better align its production with its customers. Properly structured, the swap would not result in any gain or loss.

  Stock in a company can also be considered a productive asset if the investment is accounted for under the equity method, which is generally used for stock ownerships percentages in the range of 20 percent to 50 percent. This means that certain subsidiaries may be disposed of with no gain or loss recorded.

OPERATING VERSUS NON-OPERATING INCOME

There are two basic categories of earnings: (1) operating and (2) non-operating. Operating or "core" earnings are those that are expected to continue into the future. Nonrecurring events or earnings are not expected to affect future earnings, so they are recorded as non-operating. Financial analysts typically project growth rates for core earnings, and then discount these earnings back to the present to estimate the value of a stock. GAAP facilitates this forecasting of core earnings by separating the reporting of operating and nonoperating items in the income statement.

Possible income statement categories for reporting unusual items that are not considered part of normal operating income include:

- Special or unusual charges.
- Discontinued operations.
- Extraordinary gains and losses.
- Cumulative effect of change in accounting principles.

Items in the first category are reported as a component of income from continuing operations, but the other three items are not. There are a number of gray areas in classifying some items so it is possible to manage earnings when making decisions about items falling into those areas. For example, disposition of a major manufacturing plant could possibly be classified as either a special or unusual charges or as a discontinued operations. What classification is more accurate may depend on executive judgment about factors that are discussed in the detailed GAAP requirements for reporting discontinued operations items.

EARLY RETIREMENT OF DEBT

Long-term corporate debts, such as bonds, are typically recorded at amortized book value. When they are retired early, the cash payment required may be substantially different from book value, generating an accounting gain or loss. GAAP requires this gain or loss to be reported as an extraordinary item at the bottom of the income statement even though it may not meet the normal criteria for such a classification. Executives can manage earnings by selecting the fiscal period in which they retire debt early.

Rather interestingly, GAAP also requires the reporting of an extraordinary gain or loss for early debt retirement accomplished by either debt-for-debt swaps (new bonds for old bonds) or debt-for-equity swaps (stock for outstanding bonds), even though no actual cash is actually exchanged. "Debt-for-equity swaps are used to both smooth income and to relax potentially binding sinking-fund constraints in the cheapest feasible manner." [1]

Some early debt retirements are *not* recorded as extraordinary items. These exceptions to the general rule are explained in Chapter 18.

USE OF DERIVATIVES

Derivatives are financial instruments or contracts whose value is either derived from another asset (e.g., stock, bond, or commodity) or related to a market-determined indicator (e.g., a stock market index). Derivatives can be used to protect against some types of business risk, such as:

- Interest rate changes.

---

[1] Hand, J. R. M. "Did Firms Undertake Debt-Equity Swaps For An Accounting Paper Profit or True Financial Gain?" *The Accounting Review,* Vol. LXIV No. 4, October, 1989, pp. 587-623.

- Commodity price changes.
- The weather.
- Oil price changes.
- Changes in foreign currency exchange rates.

Some of the varied types of derivatives are:

- Financial forwards (futures).
- Options.
- Swaps.[2]

The FASB concluded in 1998 that derivatives should be reported as assets and liabilities in the balance sheet and measured at fair value. Gains and losses from derivative transactions are generally recognized immediately in regular income unless they are cash flow hedges that are recorded in equity as part of comprehensive income.

Derivatives offer many opportunities to manage earnings. For example, suppose a company had a large issue of bonds outstanding at a fixed interest rate. The company could enter into an interest rate swap that would effectively convert the fixed rate bonds into variable rate bonds. When the interest rate increases, the company would then record an increase in interest expense for the bonds, and a decrease if the rate has decreased. Since when the company enters into the swap is up to the company, the timing option provides an opportunity to manage earnings.

SHRINK THE SHIP

Companies that repurchase their own shares do not have to report any gain or loss on their income statement because no income is recognized on the transaction. The reason is that, under GAAP, the company and its stock owners are considered to be one and the same. Income is only earned through equity transactions *outside* the firm, not with those involving the firm's owners.

If no gain or loss is reported on stock buybacks, how can they be used for earnings management? The answer is that although a stock buyback does not affect earnings, it *does* affect earnings per share, a widely used earnings surrogate. To briefly illustrate: Assume a company has 100,000 shares of stock outstanding and earned net income of $300,000 during the current fiscal year (see Table 2.1). The reported earning per share figure would be $3.00 ($300,000/100,000 shares). If management projects that net income will remain at $300,000 for the following fiscal year, it recognizes that this means earnings per share will be flat, rather than the average 10 percent average growth rate experienced for earnings and earnings per

---

[2] Kieso, D. E., J. J. Weygandt, and T. D. Warfield. 2001. *Intermediate Accounting*. New York: John Wiley and Sons, p. 952.

share over the last decade. If the company buys back 9,100 shares at the beginning of the next fiscal year, earnings per share for that year will $3.30—a 10 percent growth rate, even though net income remains the same.

Table 2.1. Earnings Management through Stock Repurchase

		Current Year	Next Year
Earnings			
	Earnings	$300,000	$300,000
	Rate of earnings growth	10%	0%
Earnings per share			
	Shares before and after buyback	100,000	90,900
	Earnings per share	$3.00	$3.30
	Rate of growth in earnings per share	10%	10%

3 WHY PRACTICE EARNINGS MANAGEMENT?

Motives for earnings management as well as related finance concepts underlying earnings management are explained and illustrated in this chapter.

One viewpoint about the motivation for earnings management holds that managers manage earnings primarily for their own personal security and enrichment. According to this view, they do it to:

- Maximize their compensation, including bonuses and options on stock.
- Maintain power or job security.
- Get a promotion.

A second viewpoint is that the people in charge manage earnings primarily to benefit the firm. Company interests rather than self-interest are the primary motivating factor. According to this view, they do it to:

- Maximize share price and thus company valuation.
- Minimize the probability of bankruptcy.
- Avoid violating restrictive debt covenants.
- Minimize regulatory intervention (e.g., minimizing reported profits so a company cannot be accused of price gouging or other anti-consumer behavior).

These two viewpoints do not necessarily conflict. A manager may at any one time be motivated by both personal and firm interests. Certainly it is not uncommon for executives to benefit personally if the company does well financially. An obvious occasion when personal and firm interests coincide is when an executive owns a significant number of shares in the company.

COMPENSATION TIED TO REPORTED PROFITS

Managers are typically paid a base salary plus a combination of short- and long-term incentives. The incentives are often tied to accounting numbers. For example, a contract might provide that in the short term an executive will receive a bonus of 25 percent of base salary if the company's after-tax return on assets exceeds 10 percent. A common long-term incentive is a stock option that only has value if company share prices rise above some minimum.

In one study, 47 to 55 percent of the companies surveyed used long-term performance plans involving cash or shares that were directly tied to reported accounting numbers,[1] and there were similar percentages for short-term bonus plans linkages to accounting numbers. The following accounting measures, all of which relate to net income or cash flow, are often used in compensation plans of all types:

- Cash flow.
- Return on equity.
- Return on assets.
- Earnings per share.
- Operating income or net income.
- Total shareholder return.

Given that many companies tie executive compensation to accounting results, it should be no surprise that managers attempt to manage the accounting numbers to maximize their compensation.

This phenomenon has been confirmed by numerous studies over the years. One study, looking at actions undertaken by managers when their annual bonus was tied to reported income, found that when income was expected to exceed the bonus ceiling (the point where the maximum bonus is paid), managers used discretionary accounting options to reduce earnings in the current year in order to carry the excess over into future years. In addition, when income was below the bonus threshold (the point where the bonus is triggered), managers again used their discretionary accounting options to reduce earnings even further, again to carry over earnings into future years.[2]

We can conclude, then, that many executives manage earnings because their companies give them an incentive to do so. In fact, only foolish executives would ignore reported accounting numbers when their personal compensation is dependent on those numbers. We repeat, however, that, despite personal pressure or incen-

---

[1] England, J. D. "Executive Pay, Incentives, and Performance." 1996. D. E. Logue (ed.) *Handbook of Modern Finance*. Boston: Warren, Gorham & Lamont, p. E9-3.
[2] Healy, P. "The Effect of Bonus Schemes on Accounting Decisions." *Journal of Accounting and Economics* 7 (1985): 85-108.

tives, an executive should only make those earnings management choices that are permitted by GAAP and reflect economic reality appropriately.

VALUING A COMPANY

In order to better understand the motivation to manage earnings so as to maximize share price, it is first necessary to understand how a company is valued. This section briefly explains different approaches to company valuation and presents a simple valuation model.

How do we know what a company, or a share of its stock, is worth? This is a simple question, yet it has no easy answer. There are several popular valuation models. Most of them try to determine current value by forecasting the future values of one of the following three variables:

1. Book value as per the balance sheet.
2. Operating cash flow.
3. Net income.

Book value, which is computed as assets minus liabilities, is sometimes called "net assets." Assets and liabilities are transaction residuals that result primarily from past operating, investing, and financing activities. Because book value thus reflects the past, it is usually considered more relevant for companies that do not have significant growth prospects or that are expected to be liquidated.

Economic theory tells us that in the long run total cash flow and net income will be equal. The two differ from year to year only because accrual-based accounting is mandated by GAAP. Thus, approaches that use one of these two variables are fundamentally similar, differing principally on which of the two the person making the valuation believes is most relevant. Recent empirical research indicates that stock prices correlate better with net income than with operating cash flows, so we will look at net-income-related valuations.[3]

What role does reported net income play in valuation of a company?

A theoretical answer is that the value of a company is the present value of future net income over an infinite horizon using a risk adjusted discount rate. The discount rate is usually presumed to be equal to the equity cost of capital. This may be expressed as the following model:

$$\text{Company Value} = \sum_{t=1}^{\infty} \frac{\text{Income}_t}{(1+r)^t} + \frac{\text{Income}_{t+1}}{(1+r)^{t+1}} + \frac{\text{Income}_{t+2}}{(1+r)^{t+2}} \frac{\text{Income}_{t+\infty}}{(1+r)^{t+\infty}}$$

where   t = future time period.
   r = risk adjusted discount rate (equity cost of capital).
   ∞ = infinity.

---

[3] Dechow, P. "Accounting Earnings and Cash Flows as Measures of Firm Performance: The Role of Accounting Accruals." *Journal of Accounting and Economics,* 18 (1994): 3-42.

To use this model, though, it would be necessary to estimate net income for *all* future time periods—a daunting task. Financial analysts often simplify the model by forecasting net income for five years and then making a terminal assumption for income after the end of that period, but this still leaves a somewhat complex model involving six time periods.

We can further simplify things by assuming that yearly net income will be constant in the future. This assumption leads to the following valuation model:

$$\text{Company value} = \frac{\text{Estimated future annual income}}{\text{Equity cost of capital}}$$

To illustrate this model, assume that future net income is forecast to be $1 million and the equity cost of capital is 10 percent. Given these assumptions, the model tells us that the company is worth $10,000,000 ($1,000,000/0.10).

Note that although this model estimates the overall value of a company, it can be slightly modified to estimate the value of a single share in the company. As shown below, the modified model simply uses net income expressed on a per share basis to get a per share value.

$$\text{Share value} = \frac{\text{Estimated future earnings per share}}{\text{Equity cost of capital}}$$

To illustrate, assume that future net earnings per share are forecast to be $1 and the equity cost of capital is 10 percent. Given these assumptions, the model tells us that a share in the company is worth $10 ($1/0.10).

How do we forecast the future net income? One answer is to use reported (historical) net income. For example, assume that Company A's reported net income for the past three years has been stable and no significant future changes in company operations are currently expected (see Table 3.1).

Table 3.1. Historical Reported Net Income for Company A

Year	Net Income
Two years previous	$1,000,000
One year previous	$1,000,000
Current year	$1,000,000

In this situation, we might expect that Company A's next-year net income to be $1,000,000 by a simple linear extrapolation of the past trend (see Figure 3.1).

For Company B, however, past net income has fluctuated a bit but it has still averaged $1,000,000 (see Table 3.2).

Figure 3.1. Company A: Next Year's Income as a Trend Continuation

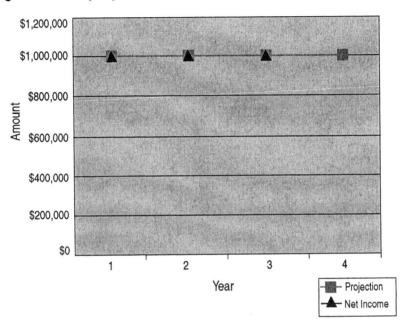

Table 3.2. Historical Reported Net Income for Company B

Year	Net Income
Two years previous	$1,200,000
One year previous	$800,000
Current year	$1,000,000

If we assume that the average past trend can be expected to continue, we might project Company B's next-year net income to be $1,000,000 by a simple linear extrapolation of the past trend (see Figure 3.2).

Would Company A and Company B both have the same value, since they both had forecasted future net incomes of $1,000,000 and identical average incomes over the recent past? From forecasted future net income alone, you might be tempted to answer yes. However, the simple valuation model has *two* factors (1) net income and (2) the risk-adjusted discount rate. Net income may be the same but the risk is not.

This deeper analysis reveals that Company A and Company B do not have the same value, even though they have the same forecasted net income, because they present different risks. Because Company A's net income is more stable than Company B's, Company A is less risky. Because it is less risky, its equity cost of capital will be less. If we assume that Company A has an equity cost of capital of 10 percent, it will be valued at $10,000,000 as previously illustrated. Due to a perceived higher risk, Company B may have an equity cost of capital of 12 percent, so it would be valued at $8,333,333 ($1,000,000/0.12).

Figure 3.2. Company B: Next Year's Income as a Trend Continuation

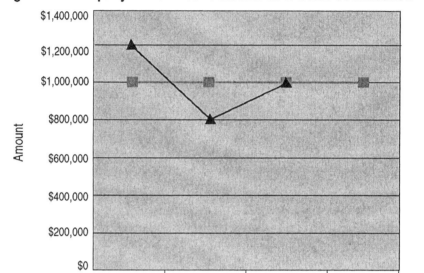

The lesson to be learned here is that *company value is penalized for earnings volatility.* Even though two companies have exactly the same forecasted earnings, one may be worth significantly more than the other.

Higher earnings volatility can affect how stakeholders assess the probability of bankruptcy, because larger up and down swings in earnings increase the chance that an extended down swing will leave the firm in a position where it cannot pay its bills, as research has proven analytically.[4]

How do we assess earnings volatility? One way is to compute the standard deviation of past earnings. The standard deviation is a common statistical measure of dispersion.

Company A had a net income standard deviation of 0 because its net income was the same for all three periods. Company B has a net income standard deviation of $200,000 due to the differences in net income in the three periods. The standard deviation gets larger as the volatility of a series of numbers increases.

Riskier investments generally have higher earnings volatility as measured by the standard deviation of annual earnings. Table 3.3 compares the standard deviation of annual returns from different classes of investments over the period from 1926 to 1993.

[4] Trueman, B., and S. Titman. "An Explanation for Accounting Income Smoothing." Journal of Accounting Research, 26 (Supplement, 1988): 127-139.

Table 3.3. Standard Deviation of Annual Returns for Different Investments Over Time

Investment	Average Return for Period 1926-1993	Standard Deviation of Returns
Treasury bills	3.7%	3.3%
Long-term Treasury bonds	5.4%	8.7%
Common stocks	12.3%	20.5%

Source: Adapted from Bodie, Z., A. Kane, and A. J. Marcus. 1996. *Investments* (3rd ed.). Flossmoor, IL: Richard D. Irwin, p. 129.

MANAGING EARNINGS TO MAXIMIZE SHARE PRICE

Company managers can sometimes eliminate some earnings volatility by careful selection of accounting methods, which helps to increase the company's share price. To illustrate this point, assume that three years ago, before the end of the fiscal year, the Company B managers from the previous example could anticipate that their net income would be $1,200,000. Because they knew this was a higher income level than Company B could probably sustain in the long run, the managers made accounting or operating choices that would reduce net income for two years previous to $1,000,000 and increase net income for the previous year one to $1,000,000. In this case, suppose management estimated on the high end of the reasonable range for cookie jar reserves in the areas of sales returns and allowances, bad debt write-offs, and inventory write-downs in order to get an additional $200,000 of expenses.

The effect of these earnings management actions would be that Company B would now have a $1,000,000 net income for all three years. It would have the same earnings volatility as Company A, and therefore the same company valuation, because its risk characteristics would be the same. However, through earnings management permitted by GAAP, Company B's managers would have increased the value of the company from $8,333,333 to $10,000,000.

This type of earnings management is sometimes called "income smoothing." To have an effect on share price, income smoothing does not have to eliminate earnings volatility totally, just reduce it. In other words, managers may be able to increase company share prices by reducing earnings volatility.

How much will the share price of a company increase due to income smoothing?

There is no good answer to this question, partly because market participants use different valuation models. Moreover, there are many other factors that can affect the equity cost of capital (the risk) used in our simple valuation model besides the smoothness of earnings. In fact, financial analysts make an assessment called "quality of earnings" that incorporates numerous factors in analyzing how good the reported current net income for a company actually is. Earnings are considered to be "perfect" if they can be used to forecast future earnings without further analysis. Earnings are less than perfect if they require a manager or financial analyst to disentangle accounting, operating, or other effects in order to make a reliable estimate of future earnings. This concept is discussed in more detail later in this book.

We *can* say, however, that absent abnormal accounting manipulations that lower the perception of quality of earnings, the share price, and thus the value of a company, will increase if the volatility of its net income over time is lowered. In other words, under normal circumstances a company with lower earnings volatility will command a higher share price.

FINANCIAL DISTRESS AND COST OF EQUITY CAPITAL

One factor that affects the equity cost of capital is the perceived degree of financial distress (the possibility of bankruptcy) that a company faces. Higher financial distress raises the equity cost of capital because equity holders demand a higher return to compensate for assuming the higher risk.

Financial distress can be evaluated using a bankruptcy prediction model. One such model was developed by McKee and Lensberg, using genetic programming, from a sample of 291 U.S. public companies over the period 1991 to 1997. The model uses three variables to produce a bankruptcy probability that ranges between 0 and 1. Using a bankruptcy probability of 0.5 as the prediction decision point, the model was 80 percent accurate in predicting bankruptcy one year before actual bankruptcy.[5]

The three variables used in the model were:

1. Company size, as measured by $\log_{10}$ (total assets/1000).

2. Profitability, as measured by net income/total assets.

3. Liquidity, as measured by cash/current liabilities.

The model was:

$$\text{Bankruptcy probability} = \frac{X^2}{X^2 + Y^2}$$

where $X =$ $(((\log_{10} \text{(total assets/1000)}) + 0.85)$
                            (net income/total assets)) - 0.85.
              $Y =$ $(1 + \text{(cash/current liabilities)})$.

---

[5] McKee, T. E., and T. Lensberg. "Genetic Programming and Rough Sets: A Hybrid Approach to Bankruptcy Classification." European Journal of Operational Research, 138 (2002): 436-451.

To illustrate the model, assume a company has the following values for the three variables:

1. $\log_{10}$ (total assets of $1 billion)/1000) = 6.

2. net income/total assets = -0.001 [a small net loss].

3. cash/current liabilities = 0.05.

Inputting the three values in the bankruptcy model would produce a bankruptcy probability of 0.40—fairly high considering that a score of 0.50 or higher would result in a forecast that the company would go bankrupt. If reasonable earnings management techniques could be used to turn the small net loss into a small net profit, say a net income/total assets ratio of 0.01, then the bankruptcy score would drop to 0.36, which is significantly moves the company away from being considered a bankruptcy risk.

ANALYSIS OF EARNINGS VOLATILITY

Financial analysts often estimate earnings volatility by computing the standard deviation of reported net income for the recent past. This analysis may involve computing the standard deviation for annual earnings or quarterly earnings.

To further illustrate the concept of managing earnings to reduce volatility, let us assume that Companies C and D have reported the annual net income amounts shown in Table 3.4.

Table 3.4.Annual Net Income Comparisons

	Net Income	
Year	Company C	Company D
1	105,000	120,000
2	98,000	83,000
3	111,090	126,090
4	104,273	89,273
5	117,551	132,551
6	110,927	95,927
7	124,405	139,405
8	117,987	102,987
9	131,677	146,677
10	125,477	110,477
Average net income	114,639	114,639
Standard deviation	10,679	21,777

Note that although the annual net income amounts are different for the two companies, the annual average net incomes for the 10 periods presented are $114,639 for both. However, though annual average net incomes are identical, the standard deviations of the annual net incomes are different. The standard deviation for Company D is approximately double that of Company C.

The reason for the difference can be seen in Figures 3.3 and 3.4. The annual net income of Company C is much more steady (i.e., less volatile than that of Company D). Though Company C net income does vary from period to period, the variation is much less than for Company D.

Figure 3.3. Company C: Confidence Interval for Net Income

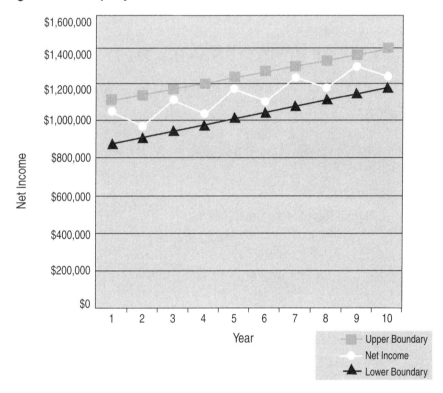

Volatility of annual net income demands attention because it affects confidence in our ability to forecast future net income, and therefore risk, in using future income to value the company. To illustrate this, Figures 3.3 and 3.4 show an upper and lower boundary computed for both companies based on a 95 percent confidence interval for forecasting future earnings. Clearly, the boundary for Company D is much wider than the boundary for Company C. This means that there is much more uncertainty, and thus more risk, in forecasting future earnings for Company

D. The boundaries for Company C cover a vertical interval of $21,627. The boundaries for Company D cover a vertical interval of $86,318. Assuming past trends continue, it will be possible to make a much more precise and less risky forecast of future earnings for Company C.

Figure 3.4. Company D: Confidence Interval for Net Income

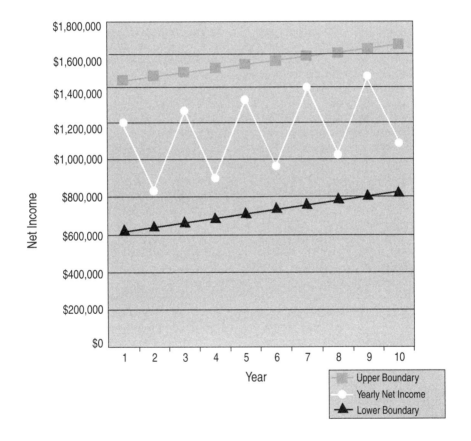

4 ETHICAL AND LEGAL CONSIDERATIONS

What factors should influence a manager's decisions about earnings management? This chapter explains some ethical, regulatory, and legal issues that an intelligent manager will consider.

Where exactly is the line between ethical and unethical earnings management? The truth is that no one knows exactly. It is a question that we all must answer for ourselves using our own ethical values. It is important, however, to think about some of the issues surrounding this question.

The results of a national survey illustrate how difficult this issue is. A questionnaire describing 13 earnings management activities that were all legal, although some were serious GAAP violations, was distributed to 649 *Harvard Business Review* readers who were general managers, finance managers, audit managers, and others in the corporate hierarchy. Respondents varied widely in their views about whether the activities were ethical.

One of the most striking findings was that none of the respondent groups were unanimous in viewing *any* one of the 13 practices as unethical. This lack of agreement on what was ethical occurred because each respondent used personal definitions of ethical and legal.[1] One conclusion from this study was that "in practice, it appears that a majority of managers use at least some methods to manage short-term earnings."[2]

Two generalizations from the study are rather interesting:

1. "On average, the respondents viewed management of short-term earnings by *accounting* methods as significantly less acceptable that accom-

[1] Bruns, W. J., and K. A. Merchant. "The Dangerous Morality of Managing Earnings." *Management Accounting,* Vol. 72, No. 2 (1990): 22-26.
[2] Ibid, p. 23.

plishing the same ends by changing or manipulating *operating decisions or procedures."*

2. *"Increasing* earnings is judged less acceptable than *reducing* earnings."[3]

ETHICAL OR MORAL DECISIONS

An ethical or moral decision is any choice where the outcome could affect the well-being of one or more individuals. Managers view an action as ethical or moral if it conforms to their own personal code of behavior or reasoning.

Ethical decisions are not necessarily the same as legal decisions. Many people apparently believe, however, that management decisions are acceptable if they are not illegal. In the words of Lester C. Thurow, then dean of the Sloan School of Management at MIT, "The question 'Is it right?' is not the same as 'Is it legal?' Yet most Americans act as if it were so."[4]

Individual ethical values or beliefs apply to all an individual's activities. They should remain constant, and not vary, for different daily activities. "Business ethics are not different from personal ethics," says Russell E. Palmer, dean of the Wharton School.[5]

Two traditional ethical systems describe the way most people think about ethics:

1. *Rule-based ethics (deontology).* Actions are viewed as ethical if they do not violate specific maximums, rules, or principles. A simplified interpretation is that if something is not expressly prohibited it is acceptable.

2. *Results-based ethics (utilitarianism).* What produces the greatest long-term good for everyone concerned is viewed as more ethical than other alternatives. This approach attempts to maximize good or right over evil or wrong.[6]

For most people, actual ethical decision making is a blend of both types of ethical systems. Often rules may not cover the specific circumstances of a particular decision. Also, most people like to justify their behavior in terms of the concept "good."

Though religion is a personal topic that many people try to keep separate from their professional lives, religion and ethics are closely intertwined. Those who have a religious foundation, therefore, have ethical values connected to theology. Conservative theology takes its ultimate authority from "divine revelation," which

---

[3] Ibid.

[4] Quoted in Albrecht, W. S. 1992. *Ethical Issues In The Practice of Accounting.*
Cincinnati, OH: South-Western Publishing Company, p. 170.

[5] Ibid., p. 167.

[6] Cottell, Jr., P. G., and T. M. Perlin. 1990. *Accounting Ethics—A Practical Guide For Professionals.* Westport, CT: Quorum Books.

means that the God for the religion has made certain truths known. Liberal theology takes its authority from reflection on human experience.

One problem in analyzing the ethics associated with earnings management is that there is no generally accepted definition of what earnings management actually is. Thus, some concepts of earnings management frame it in a bad light that may not be appropriate.

DEFINITIONS OF EARNINGS MANAGEMENT

Earnings management is usually viewed as either *a legitimate management tool* that is useful for fulfilling a manager's responsibility to maximize returns to shareholders (the position taken in this book) or *a distortion of economic events* that is misleading to some users of financial statements. These different views about earnings management lead to widely varying definitions of it. Let us look at the distortion of economic events viewpoint first.

A widely quoted 1989 definition by Schipper described earnings management as "a purposeful intervention in the external financial reporting process, with the *intent of obtaining some private gain* (as opposed to, say, merely facilitating the neutral operation of the process)" (emphasis added).[7] Schipper adopts an information perspective that considers earnings as one information signal among many that may be used in decision making. From her perspective, managers have private information they can use to influence contractual outcomes in a desired direction.

In 1999, Healy and Wahlen stated that "Earnings management occurs when managers *use judgment* in financial reporting and in structuring transactions to alter financial reports *to either mislead* some stakeholders about the underlying economic performance of the company *or* to *influence* contractual outcomes that depend on reported accounting numbers" (emphasis added).[8] The "contractual outcomes" mentioned could include either company bonus plans or stock option plans that are based on the financial statements.

There are two common aspects in these definitions. The first is that management exercises judgment in business operations and financial reporting. Everyone agrees on this. Operational decision making clearly requires judgment. GAAP clearly requires management to make estimates and judgments. Managers are paid to make good judgments. Dechow andSkinner support the view that earnings management is appropriate when managers exercise judgment:

> *"No earnings management" is clearly not an optimal solution. Some earnings management is expected and should exist in capital markets. This is necessary because of the fundamental need for judgments and*

---

[7] Schipper, K. "Commentary On Earnings Management." *Accounting Horizons,* Vol. 3, No. 4, December 1989, page 92.
[8] Healy, P. M., and J. M. Wahlen. "AReview of Earnings Management Literature and Its Implications for Standard Setting." *Accounting Horizons,* Vol. 13, No. 4, December 1999, page 368.

estimates to implement accrual accounting. . . . Eliminating all flexibility would in turn eliminate the usefulness of earnings as a measure of economic performance. "[9]

The second common aspect of the definitions given is that managers use their judgment to do such things as obtain a private gain, mislead some stockholders, or influence contractual outcomes. This views earnings management in an unnecessarily negative light. The implication is that the manager's judgment is biased. It implies that management purposefully distorts earnings either away from "true economic income" or to alter the information content. Neither of these is necessarily true in the majority of cases.

When we consider true economic income from a theoretical perspective, we find it is generally not observable (knowable) and therefore it is not something that managers can use to evaluate their decisions.[10] They would therefore find it difficult to deliberately distort income away from something that they cannot observe.

Information content is a statistical property of information that is dependent on the decision model employed. Since it is widely accepted that financial statement users employ many widely differing decision models, it should be accepted that managers do not necessarily know what specific decision model is appropriate. They would find it difficult to alter information content for a decision model not known to them. In fact:

"*. . . the FASB's Concepts Statement No. 1, paragraphs 24-30 discusses over a dozen users and uses of financial reports.* "[11]

I believe that definitions like these take an unnecessarily negative view of earnings management. A more positive definition is needed. The previous definitions are equivalent to arguing that people who shine their shoes are trying to mislead others about their appearance. It makes more sense to argue that the shoe-shining person is just putting the best foot forward. (They might be attempting to mislead if they borrowed someone else's shoes and tried to pass these off as their own!)

Arya, Glover, and Sunder argue that an appropriate earnings management analogy involves thinking about a photographer and his subject, with management being the photographer and the business being the subject. They state:

"*. . . the relationship between financial reporting and business is not like that of a photographer and a landscape. It is more like that between a*

---

[9] Dechow, P. M., and D. J. Skinner. "Earnings Management: Reconciling the Views of Accounting Academics, Practitioners, and Regulators," *Accounting Horizons*, 14 (2000): 247-248.

[10] Beaver, W., and J. Demski. "The Nature of Income Measurement." *Accounting Review*, 54 (1979): 38-46.

[11] Schipper, K., and L. Vincent. "Earnings Quality." *Accounting Horizons*, supplement, 2003, pp. 97.

photographer and a model: the model smiles and poses for the camera even as the photographer changes camera angle and settings in reaction to the model. The state of the firm and its financial reports are reflexive in the sense of being dependent on each other." [12]

Managers obviously can engage in undesirable behavior but they do not necessarily do so every time they manage earnings. Why portray everyone's motives in a negative light when many managers have positive motives? That is why this book previously used the following positive definition of earnings management:

"Reasonable and legal management decision making and reporting intended to achieve and disclose stable and predictable financial results."

This definition is intended to describe reasonable and proper practices that are part of a well-managed business that delivers value to shareholders. Earnings management is fine as long as it is not taken to extreme levels that distort the underlying financial information and therefore the picture of economic performance.

STAKEHOLDERS IN EARNINGS MANAGEMENT DECISIONS

Earnings management decisions typically affect a number of stakeholders because so many different parties rely on financial statements for decision-making. Managers should not have blinders on, seeing only one type of stakeholder when they make an earnings management decision. The following groups may be affected by such a decision:

- Employees.
- Customers.
- Suppliers.
- Creditors.
- Shareholders.
- Financial analysts.
- Stock underwriters.
- Regulators.

Many of these stakeholders have conflicting interests. A change in earnings that might be viewed as positive by one group might be viewed as negative by another. For example, suppose the chief financial officer managed earnings so as

---

[12] Arya, A., J. C. Glover, and S. Sunder. "Are Unmanaged Earnings Always Better For Shareholders?" *Accounting Horizons,* supplement 2003, p. 115.

to lower reported earnings for the current fiscal period. Employees getting ready-to negotiate a new union contract might view this negatively because it might reduce the wage increases they could realistically ask for. On the other hand, a long-term investor might view this positively if the result was that the earnings were "banked" for a future period to prevent an earnings surprise down the road.

Because these stakeholders also use different decision models, even if their general economic interests are the same they may view the effects of an earnings management decision somewhat differently. Suppose a company sold some long-term plant assets to generate a reported profit of $10,000,000 (based on book value) but realized only $1,000,000 more in cash than the mortgage on the plant had been. Creditors looking at this using a short-term cash flow decision model might see it as mildly positive, since the company would now have $1,000,000 more free cash than it previously had. Shareholders using a future earnings fore-cast model might view the same event as highly positive if the company through the sale shed itself of excess productive capacity that would be a drag on future earnings.

Penman argues that computing earnings for a variety of different stakeholders is wrong. He believes that GAAP should embrace a proprietorship perspective—that financial statements should be prepared primarily for common shareholders. The proprietorship perspective leads to somewhat different GAAP than the one currently used. Penman argues that some of the current problems with interpreting GAAP stem from the fact that it confuses the interests of the common shareholders with the interests of the firm (entity perspective).[13]

THE COMPLEXITY OF EARNINGS MANAGEMENT DECISIONS

There are typically a number of factors that must be weighed in making an earnings management decision. Each of them may reflect differing degrees of certainty, thus making the decision more difficult. Common decision factors include:

- *Size of item.* A small item may not be as significant to financial statement users.
- *Clarity of the accounting rule.* Some GAAP rules are extremely specific. Others are more general.
- *Future effect.* What effect might the current decision have on future fiscal periods?
- *Industry practices.* What are the majority of firms in the industry doing for similar items? How would a departure from the industry norm be viewed?

---

[13] Penman, S. H. "The Quality of Financial Statements: Perspectives From The Recent Stock Market Bubble.' *Accounting Horizons,* supplement, 2003, pp. 77-96.

- *Nature of the effect.* Does the earnings management action have real economic substance or is it just a change in legal form?

- *Direction of the effect.* Actions that *decrease* earnings may be viewed differently from actions that *increase* earnings.

- *Trend effect.* Earnings management actions are generally more significant if they change the direction, rate of change, or volatility of earnings trends.

- *Related disclosures.* An earnings management action that is fully disclosed might be viewed differently from one which was not. With full disclosure, knowledgeable users of financial statements can compute income under alternative assumptions.

REGULATORY CONSIDERATIONS

Many companies operate in industries where there is significant regulatory oversight. Managers of companies in these industries must consider both current and possible future regulatory interventions when making earnings management decisions. Among the industries that are significantly regulated are:

- Financial institutions.
- Public utilities.
- Telecommunications.
- Transportation.
- Health care and pharmaceuticals.
- Insurance.
- Chemicals.
- Aviation.

LEGAL CONSIDERATIONS

A wide variety of state and federal laws govern both financial reporting and financial fraud. Those who violate the law may be subject to both civil (monetary damages) and criminal (jail time) penalties if they are prosecuted.

Some of the most stringent of these laws are the federal securities statutes, starting with the 1933 and 1934 Securities and Exchange Commission Acts. These acts give considerable power over the financial markets and financial reporting to the SEC. For the 14,000 or so U.S. public companies that must register and file financial statements with the SEC, it has the power to define the form and content of financial statements and the accounting methods used to prepare them. This means that the SEC also has significant influence over the FASB processes for establishing GAAP, even though GAAP applies to private as well as public companies. The SEC normally accepts GAAP for statements filed with it.

The SEC reviews all individual financial statements filed with it and may either reject them or require their amendment if it finds a failure to follow GAAP, overly aggressive earnings management, or other reasons. The SEC often calls in criminal prosecutors when it receives information that registrants are engaged in unacceptable levels of earnings management or in fraud. For the period 1997-2002, the SEC filed 515 enforcement actions against 164 companies and 705 individuals. "Charges were brought against 75 Chairmen of the Board, 111 Chief Executive Officers (CEOs), 111 Presidents, 105 Chief Financial Officers (CFOs), 21 Chief Operating Officers (COOs), 16 Chief Accounting Officers (CAOs), and 27 vice-Presidents (VPs) of Finance."[14] (Note: The same person may have multiple titles.)

In 1998, then SEC Chairman Arthur Levitt became concerned about earnings management abuses that cross over "the gray area between legitimacy and outright fraud." He gave a series of speeches on this subject and focused the SEC on preventing earnings management abuses. This crackdown was stimulated by a string of spectacular cases over several years. The severity of the problem is suggested by a *CFO Magazine* article titled "Jailhouse Shock" that listed 22 CFOs who were either serving jail time or awaiting sentencing for fraud related financial activities.

Some of the more prominent of these were the CFOs for:

- Phar-Mar, 2 years, 9 months.
- Miniscribe, 2 years.
- California Micro Devices, 2 years 8 months.
- Cableco, 1 year 3 months.
- Lumivision, 10 years.[15]

A 1999 article in *Fortune* listed the outcomes for the CEOs of the following companies who had been nailed for accounting fraud in the previous five years:

- Underwriters Financial Group, 12 years, 1 month.
- Donnkenny, facing maximum sentence of 5 years.
- Health Management, 9 years.
- Home Theater Products Intl., 3 years, 1 month.
- FNN, 5 years.
- Crazy Eddie, 6 years, 10 months.
- Towers Financial, 20 years.[16]

---

[14] United States Securities and Exchange Commission, Report Pursuant to Section 704 of the Sarbanes-Oxley Act of 2002. January 24, 2003, pages 1-2.
http://www.sec.gov/news/studies/sox704report.pdf. Accessed December 2, 2003.
[15] Reason, T. "Jailhouse Shock." *CFO Magazine,* September 1, 2000.
[16] Loomis, L. T., "Lies, Damned Lies and Managed Earnings." *Fortune,* August 12, 1999, page 82.

Financial crime is clearly being taken more seriously today than it was 10 years ago. The average prison sentence from SEC referrals to the U.S. Attorney's offices increased from only 10 months in 1992 to 49 months in 1998.[17]

The SEC also has the power to regulate those who audit public company financial statements. Its Rules of Practice apply to accountants and auditors desiring to practice before the commission. Rule 102(e) is the basis for disciplining accountants who fail to meet these rules:

> *"The commission may deny, temporarily or permanently, the privilege of appearing or practicing before it in any way to any person who is found by the Commission after notice of opportunity for hearing in the matter (i) not to possess the requisite qualifications to represent others, or (ii) to be lacking in character or integrity or to have engaged in unethical or improper professional conduct, or (iii) to have willfully violated , or willfully aided and abetted the violation of any provision of the federal securities laws . . . , or the rules and regulations thereunder."*[18]

For the period 1997-2002, the SEC brought enforcement proceedings against 18 auditing firms and 89 individual auditors. The sanctions were stiff. One auditing firm and 24 individuals were charged with fraud under Section 10(b) of the 1934 Exchange Act.[19]

Executives pursuing legitimate earnings management goals must be aware of the legal restrictions on financial reporting and avoid extreme forms of earnings management that might be considered fraud.

FRAUD VERSUS LEGITIMATE EARNINGS MANAGEMENT

As I have said repeatedly, legitimate earnings management is reasonable and legal management decision making and reporting intended to achieve and disclose stable and predictable financial results. Fraud, on the other hand, is:

> *". . . the intentional, deliberate, misstatement or omission of material facts, or accounting data, which is misleading and, when considered with all the information made available, would cause the reader to change or alter his or her judgment or decision."*[20]

While it may sometimes be hard to determine when the line between legitimate earnings management and fraud has been crossed, we do know that the fol-

---

[17] Turner, L. E. Speech, "Opportunities for Improving Quality." *http://www.sec.gov.news/speech/spch451.htm.* Accessed October 4, 2001.
[18] Securities and Exchange Commission, *Rules of Practice,* Rule 2(e), par. 201.2.
[19] United States Securities and Exchange Commission, Report Pursuant to Section 704 of the Sarbanes-Oxley Act of 2002. Above, N. 14, pages 3 and 41.
[20] National Association of Certified Fraud Examiners, 1993, p. 12.

lowing activities would normally not be considered legitimate earnings management but rather fraud:

- Holding the sales ledger open after the end of the fiscal period so subsequent period sales are recorded in an earlier period.
- Backdating shipping documents so that it appears that items were shipped in an earlier period.
- Delaying recognition of returns sales to a later fiscal period than the one in which they were received.
- Substantially and deliberately overvaluing or undervaluing goods or services received in barter transactions.
- Recording fictitious sales.
- Failing to record legitimate expenses.
- Deliberately overvaluing or undervaluing assets.

5 SARBANES-OXLEY ACT OF 2002

This chapter explains and discusses key provisions of the Sarbanes-Oxley Act of 2002.

Financial fraud involves intentional deceit. Lack of truth creates uncertainty, and thereby risk, in the capital markets. If the uncertainty becomes widespread, then individuals will not trust and invest in the capital markets and the capital markets could collapse.

A number of spectacularly large business failures, such as Enron, have involved allegations of fraud. The negative publicity these failures created caused a loss of confidence in the capital markets. One *Newsweek* columnist reported that the Enron collapse was "the biggest crisis investors have had since 1929."[1]

To a greater extent than other scandals, "WorldCom's July, 2002, revelations—that it had carried out a scheme to disguise billions of dollars in losses by misclassifying expenses as capital expenditures—drove a reluctant White House and congressional Republicans to back a wide-ranging package of corporate and accounting reforms that became the Sarbanes-Oxley Act of 2002."[2]

The U.S. Congress responded to the clearly apparent public outrage over business failure through fraud by passing the *Sarbanes-Oxley Act of 2002 (SOA)*, which was intended to remedy perceived deficiencies in financial reporting. Knowledge of this law is highly important for anyone making earnings-related decisions. The rest of this chapter discusses key provisions of this new law.

---

[1] Byrnes, N. "Paying for the Sins of Enron." *Newsweek,* February 11, 2002, p. 35.

[2] "MCI Aims to Make WorldCom History." *Business Week* Online, May 16, 2003. *http://www.businessweek.com/bwdaily/dnflash/may2003/nf20030516_0523_db016.htm.*

HOW COMMON IS FRAUD?

The actual incidence of financial fraud reported in the United States is relatively low. T. J. F. Bishop notes that in 1999 the *Wall Street Journal* reported only 25 new cases of alleged material financial statement fraud. Given that there were 8,873 audits of public companies reported during the same period, this is a 0.003 annual fraud rate for public companies, relatively low compared to the failure rate in other professions.[3] However, the statistic addresses only the frequency of frauds, not their size and/or economic impact. It also does not include the frauds that are never discovered.

ECONOMIC IMPACT OF FRAUD

The costs of fraud can be staggering. Enron was the U.S.'s seventh largest company before it filed for bankruptcy. During 2000 it reported more than $65 billion in assets and revenues of over $100 billion. In October 2001 the firm announced that it was taking a $1.2 billion write-down of assets due to reversals of previously recorded revenue transactions. It also restated its earnings for the previous five years—eliminating approximately $591 million of previously reported profits. The loss of confidence in the firm led to the bankruptcy filing on December 2, 2001. The related decline in the Enron stock price resulted in more than $60 billion in shareholder losses.

The WorldCom fraud and subsequent bankruptcy that followed Enron were even larger. From 1999 to 2002 WorldCom booked more than $9 billion of capital expenditures as assets, thereby overstating net income. Mehta, in Fortune reported:

> *"In just a few years, WorldCom erased $200 billion in market value and shed thousands of jobs. By July 2002, the fraud and lax supervision forced WorldCom into bankruptcy."* [4]

SEC ENFORCEMENT CASES

This brief summary of some typical SEC enforcement cases should give you better insight into accounting practices that are unacceptable:[5]

- **Sensormatic Electronics Corporation.** The SEC charged the company and three senior officers with several different accounting frauds, including recording revenue in one quarter from products shipped in the next quarter. At the end of each quarter, Sensormatic turned back the computer clock that recorded and dated shipments so that out-of-period ship-

---

[3] Bishop, T. J. F. "Auditing for Fraud: Implications of Current Market Trends and Potential Responses." *Auditor's Report,* 24 (2001): 13-15.
[4] Mehta, S. M. "MCI: Is Being Good, Good Enough?" *Fortune,* October 27, 2003, p. 118.
[5] U.S. Securities and Exchange Commission, "Report Pursuant to Section 704 of the Sarbanes-Oxley Act of 2002," January 24, 2003. *http://www.sec.gov/news/studies.shtml.*

ments, and consequently revenue, would be recorded in the previous quarter. On October 11, 1995, the company filed amended financial statements for the fiscal quarter ended March 31, 1995.

- *Sunbeam Corporation.* This SEC action involved, among other things, allegations that Sunbeam had engaged in accounting fraud by improperly recognizing bill-and-hold contingency sale transactions. The SEC alleged that:
    —Sunbeam gave financial incentives to its customers to write purchase orders before they needed the goods and offered to hold the product until delivery was requested. Typically, Sunbeam also covered related costs.
    —Sunbeam improperly recorded contingent sales as revenue.
    —Just before the close of a quarter, Sunbeam allegedly booked revenue and income from purported sales to wholesalers, who incurred no expenses, accepted no ownership risks, and had the right to return unsold products.
    —On November 12, 1998, the company filed amended financial statements covering the period October 1, 1996, through March 31, 1998.

- *Cendant Corporation.* The SEC alleged that for more than 12 years senior management made topside adjustments that artificially inflated operating income by directing changes to quarterly results. Defendants allegedly reviewed and managed schedules listing fraudulent adjustments to be made to the quarterly and annual financial statements. As a result of these top-side adjustments and other frauds, pre-tax operating income reported to the public was inflated by a total of over $500 million for the period 1995 through 1997 alone. On September 29, 1998, the company filed amended financial statements covering the period January 1, 1995, through June 30, 1998.

- *Waste Management, Inc.* The SEC alleged that Waste Management improperly inflated its operating income and other measures of performance by deferring the recognition of current period operating expenses into the future and by netting one-time gains against current and prior period misstatements and current period operating expenses. Senior management increased reported operating income by understating operating expenses, making repeated fourth-quarter adjustments to improperly reduce depreciation expense on its equipment cumulatively from the beginning of the year, using a non-GAAP method of capitalizing interest on landfill development costs, failing to accrue tax and self-insurance expenses properly, improperly using purchase accounting to increase its environmental remediation reserves (liabilities), improperly charging operating expenses to the environmental remediation reserves, and failing to write-off permitting and project costs on impaired or abandoned landfills. On March 31, 1998, the company filed amended financial statements covering the period January 1, 1992, through September 30, 1997.

- *MiniScribe Corporation.* The SEC alleged that MiniScribe increased the value of its inventory by recording fictitious transfers of nonexistent inventory from its headquarters in Colorado to overseas locations. MiniScribe also allegedly repackaged scrap and obsolete inventory parts that should have been written-off and improperly included the costs in its ending inventory. The company also allegedly counted in inventory the costs of certain merchandise it had bought without recording corresponding amounts owed as liabilities. On January 2, 1990, the company filed amended financial statements covering 1986 and 1987.

- *W. R. Grace & Co.* The SEC alleged that W. R. Grace, a packaging, specialty chemical and healthcare services company, recorded liabilities through deferring income in order to build cookie-jar reserves that it later used to meet earnings estimates. W. R. Grace did not restate its consolidated financial statements. [A.A.E.R. No. 1140 (June 30, 1999)]

- *New Jersey Resources Corporation (NJR).* The Commission alleged that NJR, an energy company, failed to recognize an impairment to the carrying value of its oil and gas properties, which meant that the company's net income was overstated by $6.3 million. On April 28, 1994, the company filed amended financial statements covering the period October 1, 1992, through September 30, 1993.

- *Chester Holdings Ltd.* The SEC alleged that officers and directors overstated the value of consideration paid for five acquisitions of assets and businesses and overstated the value of the assets acquired in the Chester Holdings financial statements. For example, the officers claimed that Chester had acquired a knitting company for $14 million in stock when the fair value of the assets was worth no more than $4.9 million. On October 16, 1992, the company filed amended financial statements covering the period July 1, 1991, through June 30, 1992.[6]

OVERVIEW OF SARBANES-OXLEY

The actual title of the Sarbanes-Oxley Act, passed in July 2002, is the "Public Company Accounting Reform and Investor Protection Act." It has eleven main parts:

1. *Public Company Accounting Oversight Board (PCAOB).* It establishes a five-member board, subject to SEC oversight, to register, periodically inspect, and regulate accounting firms.

2. *Auditor independence.* It prohibits accounting firms from offering most nonaudit services to audit clients, requires that audit partners be rotated,

---

[6] Ibid.

and requires that auditors report to the audit committee of the board of directors.

3. *Corporate responsibility.* Public companies must have an independent audit committee that includes a "financial expert," and corporate officers are held responsible for financial reports and internal controls.

4. *Enhanced financial disclosure.* The SEC may set rules for disclosing off-balance sheet transactions and special purpose entities. Companies may not lend any director or officer money other than normal consumer credit. Management must assess internal controls, and have a code of ethics for senior financial officers

5. *Analyst conflicts of interest.* The SEC may promulgate rules to prevent securities analysts from having conflicts of interest.

6. *Commission resources and authority.* The act increases SEC staff and gives the SEC authority to regulate who may appear or practice before it.

7. *Studies and reports.* A number of studies on different aspects of the U.S. capital markets are commissioned.

8. *Corporate and criminal fraud and accountability.* Corporate records may not be destroyed if an investigation is underway. Auditors must retain working papers for a minimum of seven years. Whistleblowers in public companies are protected.

9. *White-collar crime penalty enhancements.* Criminal penalties for various financial crimes are toughened.

10. *Corporate tax returns.* The U.S. Congress prefers that the corporate tax return be signed by the chief executive officer.

11. *Corporate fraud and accountability.* The act increases criminal penalties for violations of securities laws, provides criminal penalties for retaliation against informants, and gives the SEC the power to prevent anyone from serving as an officer or director of a public company who has violated securities laws or regulations.

AUDITOR SERVICES PROHIBITED

To increase auditor independence from their clients, the following consulting services to audit clients are now banned totally:

- Bookkeeping and related services.
- Design and implementation of accounting systems.
- Appraisal or valuation services.
- Actuarial services.
- Internal audit outsourcing.

- Personnel services providing management or human resources.
- Investment or broker/dealer services.
- Legal services.
- Any other services that may later be regulated as impermissible.

GENERALLY ACCEPTED AUDITING STANDARDS (GAAS)

SOA Section 103 establishes the PCAOB, which has the power to establish rules, the violation of which is treated just like a violation of the 1934 Securities and Exchange Act, risking both civil and criminal penalties. It also gives the PCAOB the power to establish "generally accepted auditing standards" (GAAS), which means that the PCAOB can issue standards that must be followed by public companies.

The PCAOB has accepted the GAAS established by the American Institute of CPAs as they existed on April 16, 2003, as "Interim Auditing Standards" having the force and authority of GAAS until such time as the PCAOB may issue new standards.

SOASection 108 amended the 1933 SEC Act to clarify that the SEC has legal authority to set Generally Accepted Accounting Principles (GAAP), though it "may recognize as 'generally accepted' for purposes of the securities laws" accounting principles established by private standard-setting bodies. The standard setting body designated by the SEC to set GAAPis the FASB. To insure the independence of the FASB, it is now funded by fees collected from public companies.

MANAGEMENT RESPONSIBILITIES

SOASection 302 requires that the CEO and CFO assume corporate responsibility for a company's financial statements. These officers must sign a declaration to accompany the financial statements that states:

> *"(1) the signing officer has reviewed the report;*
>
> *(2) based on the officer's knowledge, the report does not contain any untrue statement of a material fact or omit to state a material fact necessary in order to make the statements, in light of the circumstances under which such statements were made,* **not misleading;**
>
> *(3) based on such officer's knowledge, the financial statements, and other financial information included in the report,* **fairly present in all material respects the financial condition and results of operations of the issuer.**" [7] *(emphasis added)*

---

[7] HR3763, Sarbanes-Oxley Act of 2002, Section 302, *www.findlaw.com.*

The provision was intended to remind managers that they are primarily responsible for making sure the financial statements conform to GAAP. It is generally presumed that, in normal circumstances, GAAP ensures that statements are not misleading and fairly present, in all material respects, the financial condition of a company.

SAMPLE SECTION 302 RESPONSIBILITY STATEMENT

The following SOA certification by Steven A. Ballmer, CEO of Microsoft Corporation was included in the 10-K filing for fiscal year ended June 30, 2003:

"Exhibit 31.1

CERTIFICATIONS

I, Steven A. Ballmer, certify that:

1. I have reviewed this annual report on Form 10-K of Microsoft Corporation;

2. Based on my knowledge, this report does not contain any untrue statement of a material fact or omit to state a material fact necessary to make the statements made, in light of the circumstances under which such statements were made, not misleading with respect to the period covered by this report;

3. Based on my knowledge, the financial statements, and other financial information included in this report, fairly present in all material respects the financial condition, results of operations and cash flows of the registrant as of, and for, the periods presented in this report;

4. The registrant's other certifying officer and I are responsible for establishing and maintaining disclosure controls and procedures (as defined in Exchange Act Rules 13a-15(e) and 15d-15(e)) for the registrant and have:

a) Designed such disclosure controls and procedures, or caused such disclosure controls and procedures to be designed under our supervision, to ensure that material information relating to the registrant, including its consolidated subsidiaries, is made known to us by others within those entities, particularly during the period in which this report is being prepared;

b) Evaluated the effectiveness of the registrant's disclosure controls and procedures and presented in this report our conclusions about the effectiveness of the disclosure controls and procedures, as of the end of the period covered by this report based on such evaluation; and

c) Disclosed in this report any change in the registrant's internal control over financial reporting that occurred during the registrant's most recent fiscal quarter (the registrant's fourth fiscal quarter in the case of an annual report) that has materially affected, or is reasonably likely to materially affect, the registrant's internal control over financial reporting; and

5. The registrant's other certifying officer and I have disclosed, based on our most recent evaluation of internal control over financial reporting, to the registrant's auditors and the audit committee of registrant's board of directors (or persons performing the equivalent functions):

a) All significant deficiencies and material weaknesses in the design or operation of internal control over financial reporting which are reasonably likely to adversely affect the registrant's ability to record, process, summarize and report financial information; and

b) Any fraud, whether or not material, that involves management or other employees who have a significant role in the registrant's internal control over financial reporting.

Date: September 4, 2003

/s/ Steven A. Ballmer

Steven A. Ballmer
Chief Executive Officer"[8]

---

[8] *http://www.sec.gov/Archives/edgar/data/789019/000119312503045632/dex311.htm.* Accessed November 5, 2003.

FINANCIAL PAYBACK PROVISIONS

SOA Section 304 provides that if a company is required to file restated financial statements due to "misconduct related to material noncompliance," the CEO and CFO must return:

- Any bonus or incentive compensation received during the 12-month period after the filing.
- Profits from sales of stock during that 12-month period.

This section was intended to prevent executives from reaping personal rewards based on company financial statements that contain material misstatements.

On November 5, 2003, an Associated Press article reported that Richard Scrushy had become the first executive indicted under the Sarbanes-Oxley Act of 2002:

> *"Richard Scrushy, the former chief executive of HealthSouth Corp., was indicted in a $2.7 billion accounting fraud. Scrushy, 51, pleaded innocent to 85 counts—including fraud, conspiracy and money-laundering."*[9]

According to the article, the charges against Scrushy carry a potential total punishment of 650 years in prison and fines of $36 million. The indictment also seeks to recover an additional $278 million of ill-gotten gains, presumably under SOA Section 304.

MICROSOFT CODE OF ETHICS EXAMPLE

The following code of conduct was obtained from the Microsoft corporate Web site. As noted in the last paragraph, this code is intended to comply with Section 406 of the Sarbanes-Oxley Act:

```
"Microsoft Finance Code of Professional Conduct
```

- ```
  Microsoft Finance's mission includes promotion of
  professional conduct in the practice of financial
  management worldwide. Microsoft's Chief Executive
  Officer (CEO), Chief Financial Officer (CFO),
  Corporate Controller and other employees of the
  finance organization hold an important and elevated
  role in corporate governance in that they are
  uniquely capable and empowered to ensure that all
  stakeholders' interests are appropriately balanced,
  protected and preserved. This Finance Code of
  ```

---

[9] *The Post and Courier,* Charleston, South Carolina, November 5, 2003, p. 9B.
  ```

Professional Conduct embodies principles to which we are expected to adhere and advocate. These tenets for ethical business conduct encompass rules regarding both individual and peer responsibilities, as well as responsibilities to Microsoft employees, the public and other stakeholders. The CEO, CFO and Finance organization employees are expected to abide by this Code as well as all applicable Microsoft business conduct standards and policies or guidelines in Microsoft's employee handbook relating to areas covered by this Code. Any violations of the Microsoft Finance Code of Professional Conduct may result in disciplinary action, up to and including termination of employment.

- All employees covered by this Finance Code of Professional Conduct will:
  —Act with honesty and integrity, avoiding actual or apparent conflicts of interest in their personal and professional relationships.
  —Provide stakeholders with information that is accurate, complete, objective, fair, relevant, timely and understandable, including in our filings with and other submissions to the U.S. Securities and Exchange Commission.
  —Comply with rules and regulations of federal, state, provincial and local governments, and other appropriate private and public regulatory agencies.
  —Act in good faith, responsibly, with due care, competence and diligence, without misrepresenting material facts or allowing one's independent judgment to be subordinated.
  —Respect the confidentiality of information acquired in the course of one's work except when authorized or otherwise legally obligated to disclose.
  —Confidential information acquired in the course of one's work will not be used for personal advantage.
  —Share knowledge and maintain professional skills important and relevant to stakeholder's needs.

—Proactively promote and be an example of ethical behavior as a responsible partner among peers, in the work environment and the community.
—Achieve responsible use, control, and stewardship over all Microsoft assets and resources that are employed or entrusted to us.
—Not unduly or fraudulently influence, coerce, manipulate, or mislead any authorized audit or interfere with any auditor engaged in the performance of an internal or independent audit of Microsoft's financial statements or accounting books and records.

- If you are aware of any suspected or known violations of this Code of Professional Conduct, the Standards of Business Conduct or other Microsoft policies or guidelines, you have a duty to promptly report such concerns either to your manager, another responsible member of management, a Human Resources representative, an LCA contact or the Director of Compliance or the 24-hour Business Conduct Line. The procedures to be followed for such a report are outlined in the Standards of Business Conduct and the Whistleblowing Reporting Procedure and Guidelines in the Employee Handbook.

- If you have a concern about a questionable accounting or auditing matter and wish to submit the concern confidentially or anonymously, you may do so by sending an e-mail to (msft.buscond@alertline.com), calling the Business Conduct Line 24-hour number at 1-877-320-MSFT (6738) or International Toll Free number at 1-704-540-0139. You may also send a letter or fax reporting your concern to Microsoft's Director of Compliance.

- Microsoft will handle all inquiries discretely and make every effort to maintain, within the limits allowed by law, the confidentiality of anyone requesting guidance or reporting questionable behavior and/or a compliance concern.

- It is Microsoft's intention that this Code of
  Professional Conduct be its written code of ethics
  under Section 406 of the Sarbanes-Oxley Act of
  2002, complying with the standards set forth in
  Securities and Exchange Commission Regulation S-K
  Item 406."[10]

INDEPENDENT AUDITORS

SOA Section 303 makes it illegal for any officer or director to:

". . . take any action to fraudulently influence, coerce, manipulate, or mislead any independent public or certified accountant engaged in the performance of an audit of the financial statements of that issuer."[11]

This means that management must fully disclose all relevant information to the independent auditors and not try to conceal corporate information from them. Management is also prohibited from pressuring auditors to permit or overlook questionable accounting practices.

SOA Section 204 requires independent auditors to report to the board of directors audit committee:

"(1) all critical accounting policies and practices to be used.

(2) all alternative treatments of financial information within generally accepted accounting principles [GAAP] that have been discussed with management . . . ramifications of the use of such alternative disclosures and treatments, and the treatment preferred . . . by the CPA firm.

(3) other written communications between the registered accounting firm and the management . . . such as any management letter or schedule of unadjusted differences."[12]

The practical significance of Section 204 is that even if management obtains the consent of independent auditors with respect to the GAAP applied to the financial statements, the audit committee of the board must still be fully informed about accounting principle alternatives.

[10] *http://www.microsoft.com/msft/governance/financecode.mspx.* Accessed November 05, 2003.
[11] HR3763, Sarbanes-Oxley Act of 2002, Section 303, *www.findlaw.com.*
[12] HR3763, Sarbanes-Oxley Act of 2002, Section 204, *www.findlaw.com.*

6 RESEARCH ABOUT EARNINGS MANAGEMENT

This chapter discusses a wide variety of research on earnings management.

It should be no surprise that there is a long line of academic research on different aspects of earnings management. Some of the research is inconclusive. It leaves us wondering. Other research is fairly definitive. It provides insights that executives will want to take into account. Some of the most significant questions are discussed here.

WHEN FIRMS ENGAGE IN EARNINGS MANAGEMENT

A 1994 study by Perry and Williams that examined 175 management buyouts during the period 1981-1988 found that unexpected accounting accruals (recording income or expense before actual cash flow) tended to decrease income before a management buyout.[1] This finding was supported by a more recent study by Marquardt and Wiedman, who examined 45 management buyouts during the period 1996-1998 and found "revenues are managed downwards prior to management buyouts."[2] Stated simply, accounting methods were employed to *lower earnings* before management buyouts.

---

[1] Perry, S., and T. Williams. "Earnings Management Preceding Management Buyout Offers." *Journal of Accounting and Economics,* 18 (1994): 157-179.
[2] Marquardt, C. A., and C. I. Wiedman. "How Are Earnings Managed? An Examination of Specific Accruals." Unpublished draft (January 2001), p. 20.

Several studies in 1998 and 1999 indicate that accruals tend to increase earnings before equity stock offerings or stock financed acquisitions.[3,4] This is confirmed by the Marquardt and Wiedman study, previously cited, which found that in their overall sample of 4,187 firms, for the 1,601 firms making equity offerings, discretionary accruals were more positive (income-increasing). When these accruals were later reversed, earnings declined. This may partially explain why research shows that initial public offerings (IPOs) are systematically overpriced.

Burgstahler and Eames found that executives manage earnings to meet analysts' forecasts. Earnings were managed upwards to avoid falling short of analysts' expectations.[5] Their findings were supported by a 1999 study by Kasznik[6] and the 2001 study by Marquardt and Wiedman.[7]

A 2003 study of Belgian companies found that both private and public companies engaged in earnings management and income smoothing. The study also found less constraint by auditors on the earnings management process for companies whose earnings were below target levels. It was hypothesized that the low level of litigation in Belgium influenced the auditors' actions. This study confirms earnings management exists outside the United States, but that the environment within a country influences how and what is done.[8]

Clearly, firms may engage in earnings management to manage earnings either up or down, depending on the management incentives that may be present. This conclusion is supported by a theoretical model recently created by Koch and Wall. In their model executives maximize their compensation by using accruals to manage earnings. The agents in their model included a manager, the firm's board of directors, and an auditor. Any of four strategies were possible, depending on factors such as managerial compensation contract, managerial time preferences, and whether perceived latent (true) earnings were above or below target:

- *Income smoothing.* Increase or decrease earnings as necessary, using discretionary accruals to attain a target net income.
- *Occasional big bath.* Where it is not possible to use discretionary accru-

---

[3] Teoh, S. H., T. J. Wong, and G. Rao. "Are Accruals During Initial Public Offerings Opportunistic?" *Review of Accounting Studies,* 3 (1998): 175-208.

[4] Erickson, M., and S. W. Wang. "Earnings Management By Accounting Firms In Stock For Stock Mergers." *Journal of Accounting and Economics,* April 1999, Vol. 27, pp. 149-176.

[5] Burgstahler, D., and M. Eames. "Management of Earnings and Analysts Forecasts." 1998. Working Paper, University of Washington, College of Business.

[6] Kasznik, R. "On the Association Between Voluntary Disclosure and Earnings Management." *Journal of Accounting Research,* 37 (1999): 57-82.

[7] Op cit., n. 2.

[8] Bauwhede, H. V., M. Willekens, and A. Gaeremynck. "Audit Firm Size, Public Ownership, and Firms' Discretionary Accruals Management." *International Journal of Accounting,* Vol. 38, 2003, pp. 1-22.

als to obtain target net income, take the largest write-off possible, thereby reporting the lowest net income possible.

- *Live for today.* Always minimize discretionary accruals, thus maximizing reported net income.
- *Maximize variability.* Use discretionary accruals to increase or decrease earnings as needed to move earnings *away* from target net income.[9]

THE MOST BENEFICIAL EARNINGS GOALS

Numerous studies document the incentives for executives to manage earnings.[10] Degeorge and colleagues provide evidence that the following hierarchy exists for the three most common earnings goals:

1. Avoid losses.
2. Report increases in quarterly earnings.
3. Meet analysts' earnings forecasts.[11]

Loss avoidance is the most important because losses can cause a large negative reaction in stock prices. Thus, executives focus first on avoiding reporting red ink. If losses cannot be avoided, executives should consider taking a big bath to clear the deck for future profitability. The big bath technique is discussed in detail in Chapter 10.

Once a firm achieves profitability, its next goal is to report regular increases in quarterly earnings. A steady pattern of earnings increases will have a favorable impact on stock prices. Several studies indicate "that firms reporting continuous growth in annual earnings are priced at a premium to other firms, that this premium increases with the length of the string, and that the premium is reduced when the string disappears."[12] In line with this conclusion, DeAngelo, DeAngelo, and Skinner report that New York Stock Exchange firms that had reported at least nine consecutive increases in annual earnings suffered market adjusted stock price declines of 15 percent in the year this string was broken.[13]

When the second goal has been met, management can turn to the goal of meeting analysts' earnings forecasts. This can be achieved either by managing earnings or by influencing analysts' forecasts through such management actions as releas-

---

[9] Koch, T. W., and L. D. Wall. "The Use of Accruals to Manage Reported Earnings: Theory and Evidence." Working Paper 2000-23 (November 2000). Atlanta: Federal Reserve Bank.

[10] Dechow, P. M., and D. J. Skinner. "Earnings Management: Reconciling the Views of Accounting Academics, Practitioners, and Regulators." *Accounting Horizons,* 14 (2000): 242-43.

[11] Degeorge, R., J. Patel, and R. Zechhauser. "Earnings Management to Exceed Thresholds." *Journal of Business,* 72 (1999): 1-33.

[12] Op. cit., n. 10, p. 244.

[13] DeAngelo, H., L. DeAngelo, and D. J. Skinner. "Reversal of Fortune: Dividend Policy and the Disappearance of Sustained Earnings Growth." *Journal of Financial Economics,* 1996, Vol. 40, pp 341-371.

ing information, positive or negative, about current business activities or future expectations.[14]

STOCK MARKET RECOGNITION OF EARNINGS MANAGEMENT

Hand found that investors are not naïve. They recognized that reported earnings declined when companies adopted LIFO inventory methods during periods of inflation to minimize taxes.[15]

Numerous studies of loan loss accruals in the banking industry showed that stock returns were negatively related to normal changes in loan loss provisions but positively related to abnormal loan loss provisions. In other words, stock prices went down when loan loss provisions (accruals) were normal and went up when loan loss provisions were above normal:

> *"One interpretation . . . is that investors . . . suspect that firms with abnormally low loan loss provisions are managing earnings upward and discount their reported performance accordingly."[16]*

In other words, investors recognized when earnings were being managed.

On the other hand, research investigating earnings management when firms issue additional shares found that firms with income-increasing abnormal accruals in the year of equity offering had significant underperformance in their stock price in subsequent years.[17] This might be interpreted to mean that users of financial statements did not recognize the effects of the earnings management at the time they occurred.

A 1996 study by Dechow and Sweeney found that firms subject to SEC investigations for earnings management suffered a 9 percent stock price decrease when the investigations were announced.[18] This suggests that investors had not recognized the earnings management before the SEC investigation.

Beneish and Vargus examined 3,906 firms over the period 1985-1996. They found that "investors price all positive accruals as if they were informative."[19] In

---

[14] Op. cit., n. 10, p. 243.

[15] Hand, J. R. M. "Resolving LIFO Uncertainty: A Theoretical and Empirical Examination of 1974-1975 Adoptions and Non-Adoptions." *Journal of Accounting Research,* 31 (1992): 21-49.

[16] Healy, P. M., and J. M. Wahlen. "A Review of Earnings Management Literature and Its Implications for Standard Setting." *Accounting Horizons,* 13 (1999): 373.

[17] Teoh, S. H., I. Welch, and T. J. Wong. "Earnings Management of the Post-Issue Performance of Seasoned Equity Offerings." *Journal of Financial Economics,* 50 (1998): 63-99.

[18] Dechow, P. M., R. G. Sloan, and A. P. Sweeney. "Causes and Consequences of Earnings Manipulation: An Analysis of Firms Subject to Enforcement Actions by the SEC." *Contemporary Accounting Research,* 13 (1996): 1-36.

[19] Beneish, M. D., and M. E. Vargus. "Insider Trading, Earnings Quality, and Accrual Mispricing." *Accounting Review,* 4 (2002): 755-791.

other words, investors mispriced some of the positive accruals because they treated them all as if they were valid information about the direction of earnings, when in fact some of them were not. Negative accruals were not found to be mispriced.

In summary, research appears to be mixed on the question of whether the stock market recognizes earnings management when it occurs. One interpretation is that investors are able to recognize some forms of earnings management but not others. Another possible interpretation that is consistent with the research stream is that investors may be able to recognize earnings management but are not always sure how much effect it has on earnings. The capital markets may adjust the stock price for an expected amount of earning management, but they can be surprised and adjust the price downward if the earnings management is larger than expected.

The latter interpretation is supported by the work of Sloan, who found that market participants overestimate the persistence of low-quality of earnings while they underestimate the persistence of high quality earnings.[20] Dechow and Skinner conclude that studies by Sloan and others "suggest that market participants are 'fooled'by relatively simple (and transparent) earnings management practices."[21]

MARKET PENALTIES FOR "EXCESSIVE" EARNINGS MANAGEMENT

Earnings management may be considered excessive, as already noted, if it is overly aggressive or fraudulent. At that point management has crossed the line beyond what would be considered a reasonable management action supported by GAAP.

Dechow, Sloan, and Sweeney examined the stock market reaction to firms that were publicly identified due to SEC enforcement actions as having manipulated earnings. They found the following four negative outcomes:

- Increase in bid-ask spreads on stock price.
- Decline in number of analysts following the stock.
- Increase in dispersion of analyst forecast errors.
- Increase of interest in stock by short sellers.[22]

The public accusation that management has engaged in earnings management to the degree that could be regarded as excessive reduces the credibility of management disclosures. It may also signal to investors that management was motivated to take this action because the firm had poor economic prospects.

---

[20] Sloan, R. G. "Do Stock Prices Fully Reflect Information In Accruals and Cash Flows About Future Earnings?" *Accounting Review,* 71 (1996): 289-315.
[21] Dechow, P. M., and D. J. Skinner. "Earnings Management: Reconciling the Views of Accounting Academics, Practitioners, and Regulators." *Accounting Horizons,* 14 (2000): 246.
[22] Op. cit., n. 18, 1-36.

THE ROLE OF AUDITORS

Auditors are supposed to be the watch dogs that protect financial statement users. That is why there are detailed auditing standards and ethical requirements to govern how they audit. These standards state that auditors can only give a "clean" opinion when they are satisfied the financial statements "present fairly" the financial results in accordance with GAAP.

If during their examination auditors question either the amount or reporting of an item, they must discuss the item with managers to try to convince them to change the financial statements. Auditors cannot change the financial statements themselves because the statements are a management product. Auditors can only change their opinion on the financial statements.

During discussion of a questionable item, managers have the opportunity to convince the auditors that the accounting treatment is acceptable. If they are successful, the auditors accept the item as reported in the financial statement. If not, auditors may issue some type of opinion other than a "clean" one. This modified opinion will bring attention to the item in question. Research suggests that modified audit opinions may have a negative impact on the stock price. This gives the auditor considerable leverage in discussions with management.

One factor that affects these discussions is the concept of *materiality.* A financial statement item is material if it might affect the decision processes of a user of the financial statement. Auditors will not modify audit opinions for items they do not consider material. Although materiality is a complex concept, a widely used quantitative rule of thumb is that items that are less than 3 to 5 percent of net income are so small that they will not be considered material.

Nelson, Elliott, and Tarpley examined how auditors interact with company executives who are managing earnings. They examined 526 earnings management attempts that were identified by surveying audit managers and partners from one Big 5 accounting firm. For this large number of earnings management attempts they found:

- Twenty-two percent were accepted because auditors believed they were permitted by GAAP.
- Eighteen percent were accepted because the auditors had no convincing evidence that the client's position was incorrect.
- Seventeen percent were accepted for a variety of other reasons but usually because the auditors thought the effects were immaterial.
- Forty-three percent were questioned by the auditors, who required their clients to adjust the financial statements.

Thus, 57 percent of earnings management attempts were permitted by the auditors.[23]

---

[23] Nelson, M. W., J. A. Elliott, and R. L. Tarpley. "Where Do Companies Attempt Earnings Management, and When Do Auditors Prevent It?" October 22, 2000 draft.

7 QUALITY OF EARNINGS

This chapter explains how the "quality of earnings" concept can affect a company's stock price and, which earnings management techniques are most useful in ensuring good quality earnings.

The quality of earnings concept is very important to the company's stock price. A good understanding of the concept will help an executive to do a better job in selecting earnings management techniques that benefit the company.

THE ROLE OF ACCOUNTING IN CORPORATE VALUATION

Corporate valuation at its simplest is merely estimating the intrinsic value of stock using some financial measure. As already mentioned, the most common financial measures used to estimate stock value are:

- Book value.
- Operating cash flow.
- Net income (earnings).

Since all these measures are based on standards for recording accounting transactions, accounting principles play a primary role in corporate valuation.

Valuations based on book value look at the underlying corporate assets and liabilities. This type of valuation is primarily useful for companies that have no growth prospects or that expect to be liquidated. Earnings do not play a significant role.

The operating cash flow valuation model is based on estimating future cash flows and then discounting them to the present using an appropriate cost of capital. This would presumably be the preferred model because it is supported by an extensive amount of economic theory, but the cash flow model is not as practical as the net income model, which is based on current earnings.

EARNINGS-BASED VALUATION

The operating cash flow model and the net income model are very similar. They differ only in the timing and nature of the underlying flow they use. Because the net income model is based on accrual accounting principles, it is more forward looking than the operating cash flow model.

The forward-looking nature of accrual accounting can be illustrated by thinking about how accrual and cash basis accounting would differ in the following situation:

- On the last day of fiscal Year 1, a magazine company received $3 million in cash for subscriptions to be filled over Years 2, 3, and 4 (the next three years) by mailing magazines monthly.

Under the cash basis of accounting, $3 million in revenue would be recorded on the day the cash was received, even though no magazines had actually been shipped. Cash basis accounting only looks at the day of the transaction, not into the future.

Under the accrual basis of accounting, no revenue would be recorded when the money was received. Instead, the $3 million would be recognized ratably over the next three years as the magazines shipped. Accrual accounting looks past the day of the transaction into the future. Accrual accounting is forward looking.

Figure 7.1 illustrates for this transaction the differences in the timing of revenue recognition between cash and accrual accounting.

Accrual accounting takes a long-horizon, multiple-period approach to computing earnings. This is useful in predicting future earnings to be used in predicting future cash flows. Current earnings provide the basis for estimating these future cash flows Stock price can then be determined based on the predicted cash flows. Figure 7.2 shows these linkages.

The belief that accrual-based earnings are more useful for assessing performance than current cash flows is supported by the FASB, the rule making body that formulates GAAP:

> *"Information about enterprise earnings and its components measured by accrual accounting generally provides a better indication of enterprise performance than information about current cash receipts and payments."*[1]

---

[1] "Objectives of Financial Reporting by Business Enterprises." *Statement of Financial Accounting Concepts* No. 1. Stamford, CT: FASB, 1978, paragraph 43.

Figure 7.1. Cash Basis versus Accrual Basis

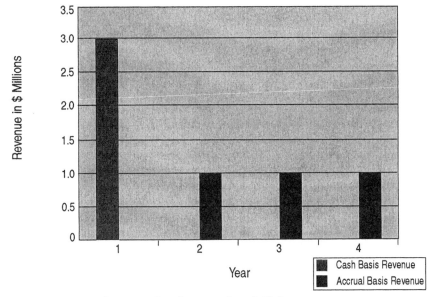

Figure 7.2. From Current Earnings to Stock Price

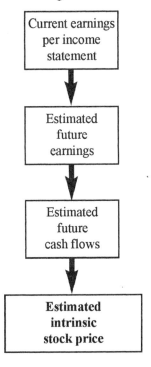

This statement is supported by empirical research that shows two results:

1. Current earnings forecast future cash flows better than current cash flows do.[2]
2. Stock prices relate more closely to accrual earnings than to current cash flows from operations.[3]

Interestingly, what accrual accounting (GAAP) does is to smooth the underlying cash flows through the use of accruals and deferrals to match revenue with related expenses. Revsine, Collins, and Johnson in a leading textbook, make the following comment supporting this view:

> *"Through the use of accruals and deferrals, accrual accounting produces an earnings number that smoothes out the unevenness or "lumpiness" in year-to-year cash flows, and it provides an estimate of sustainable "annualized" long-run future free cash flows."[4]*

The smoothed earnings produced by accrual accounting (GAAP) are only useful in predicting future earnings when they are of high quality and are sustainable. This is where the concept of quality of earnings comes in.

WHAT IS "QUALITY OF EARNINGS"?

Current earnings are useful because they can be used to forecast future earnings. "Quality of earnings" refers simply to how well they do that. Current earnings are low quality if they have a low correlation with future earnings and high quality if the correlation is high. Obviously the higher the earnings quality, the better the future earnings forecast. In fact, earnings quality can even on occasion be considered "perfect." This would mean that the coefficient of correlation was 1.0.

Current earnings are considered "perfect" if they can be expected to grow at equity cost of capital, adjusted for net dividends, with future residual earnings expected to be the same as current residual earnings.[5] This occurs when current earnings can be multiplied by a normal price-earnings ratio to obtain an intrinsic stock valuation. For example, if current earnings for a company are $1 a share and this is multiplied by a normal price-earnings ratio of 12 to obtain a stock valuation of $12, and if $12 was in fact the intrinsic value of the stock, then earnings of $1 would be "perfect."

---

[2] Barth, M., D. Cram, and K. Nelson. "Accruals and the Prediction of Future Cash Flows." *Accounting Review,* Vol. 76, No. 1 (2001): 27-58.

[3] Dechow, P. "Accounting Earnings and Cash Flows as Measures of Firm Performance: The Role of Accounting Accruals." *Journal of Accounting and Economics,* 18 (1994): 3-42.

[4] Revsine, L., D. W. Collins, and W. B. Johnson. 2002. *Financial Reporting and Analysis* (2nd ed.). Upper Saddle River, NJ: Prentice Hall, p. 237.

[5] Penman, S. H. 2001. *Financial Statement Analysis and Security Valuation.* New York: McGraw-Hill Irwin, p. 531.

FACTORS AFFECTING QUALITY OF EARNINGS

There is no consensus on exactly how to measure earnings quality. Penman cites five factors affecting earnings quality:

1. *GAAP quality.* Has the company selected the best accounting methods from those available?

2. *Audit quality.* Have the auditors detected all misstatements, intentional or unintentional, and determined that GAAP was proper?

3. *GAAP application quality.* Have the accounting methods been used appropriately and consistently?

4. *Business transaction quality.* Do the recorded business transactions have real economic substance and are they properly represented?

5. *Disclosure quality.* Do the footnotes and other disclosures provide the information an investor needs to fully understand earnings?[6]

These components are sometimes separated into two groups, accounting-related and operations-related. If management chose depreciable lives for machinery that were significantly longer than industry averages, with no linkage to actual physical or technological obsolescence of the machinery, this would be an accounting-related component of earnings. It would lower earnings quality because the lower depreciation deduction due to the longer life would increase current earnings to an amount that would be higher than is sustainable in the long run.

An operations-related component of earnings could be a decision by management to significantly cut advertising expenditures in order to increase earnings for the current period. These earnings, presumably, would not be sustainable in the absence of continued heavy advertising.

Thus, a key element of earnings quality is whether earnings are *sustainable*— whether they can be expected to continue into the future. If they are, then they correlate better with future earnings. Sustainable earnings are those:

"... *generated from repeat customers or from a high quality product that enjoys steady customer demand based on clear brand name identity. Examples of unsustainable earnings items include gains and losses from debt retirement; asset write-offs from corporate restructuring and plant closings; or temporary reductions in discretionary expenditures for advertising, research and development, or employee training.*"[7]

---

[6] Ibid., p. 599.
[7] Op. cit., n. 4, p. 245.

ONE BENCHMARK OF EARNINGS QUALITY

Although financial analysts recognize that there are many factors that affect quality of earnings, they still use simple benchmarks to assess earnings quality. One that is widely used is:

Earnings quality benchmark = Cash flow from operations/Net income.

For a company that reported net income of $2 million but only had $1 million of cash flow from operations, the earnings quality benchmark would be 0.5 (0.5 = $1/$2). On the other hand, a company with net income of $2 million and cash flow from operations of $2 million would have an earnings quality benchmark of 1 (1 = $2/$2).

As the benchmark approaches 1, the higher the earnings quality. A simplified explanation would be that if a company is able to collect in cash all the revenue it has recorded, it is more likely that revenue stream will persist into the future. "Put another way, a company with a high level of net income and a low cash flow may be using income recognition or expense accrual criteria that are suspect."[8]

ASSESSING COMPREHENSIVE EARNINGS QUALITY

According to *Business Week,* in 2001 Trevor Harris, an accounting analyst at Morgan Stanley, assembled a set of 23 earnings quality checks, among them such things as the number of one-time charges against earnings and the earnings quality benchmark just discussed. Another analyst applied these criteria to two computer service companies with the following result, on a 10 point scale with a higher score being better:

Company	Ticker Symbol	P/E Ratio	Earnings Quality Score
Electronic Data Systems	EDS	7	3.2
Fiserv Inc.	FISV	23	8.2

The report in *Business Week* stated:
> *"The message here: The higher the quality of earnings, the better valuation the market will give the company."*[9]

While there is no disputing that conclusion, it should be noted that a variety of factors other than earnings quality, such as the expected future growth rate, also influence the P/E ratio. Consequently, it is difficult to know just how much effect earnings quality has on the P/E ratio.

---

[8] Bernstein, L. 1993. *Financial Statement Analysis* (5th ed.). Homewood, IL: Irwin, p. 461.
[9] Henry, D. "Cleaning Up the Numbers." *Business Week,* March 24, 2003.

EARNINGS COMPONENTS

One way to analyze current earnings is to break them into three components:

1. *Permanent earnings.* These are expected to be sustainable, persisting into the future. They could be valued by multiplying them by a normal P/E ratio.

2. *Transitory earnings.* These result from one-time events or transactions and are not expected to be sustainable. They are nevertheless real earnings that contribute to the wealth of the firm. They could be valued by a P/E multiple of 1.

3. *Value-irrelevant earnings.* Because these are unrelated to future earnings or future cash flows, they are not related to current stock valuation. These earnings have no real economic substance and do not contribute to the wealth of the firm. They could be valued by a P/E multiple of 0.[10]

The three earnings components correspond roughly to the three major sections in a multiple-step income statement:

Permanent earnings	Income from continuing operations (with the possible exception of special items).
Transitory earnings	Income (loss) from discontinued operations and extraordinary gains and losses.
Value-irrelevant earnings	Change in accounting principle that gives rise to a cumulative effect adjustment.[11]

FROM EARNINGS COMPONENTS TO STOCK VALUATION

I said earlier that if a company's current earnings of $1 per share were multiplied by a normal price-earnings ratio of 12 to obtain a stock valuation of $12, and $12 was in fact the intrinsic value of the stock, then the earnings of $1 would be "perfect." But suppose analysis of current earnings of $1 per share indicates they are 70 percent permanent, 20 percent transitory, and 10 percent value-irrelevant. In that case the stock valuation could be computed as shown in Table 7.1.

---

[10] Ramakrishnan, R., and J. Thomas. "Valuation of Permanent, Transitory, and Price-Irrelevant Components of Reported Earnings." *Journal of Accounting, Auditing, and Finance,* 13 (1998): 301-336.
[11] Op. cit., no. 4, pp. 242-243.

Table 7.1. Computing Stock Value with Different Earnings Components

A	B	C	D	E	F
Component	*Earnings Percentage for*	*Earnings Per Share*	*Earnings Per Share for Component {D=B*C}*	*Price/ Earnings Multiplier*	*Estimated Future Value of Earnings {F=D*E}*
Permanent	70%	$1	$ 0.70	12	$8.40
Transitory	20%	$1	$ 0.20	1	$0.20
Value-irrelevant	10%	$1	$ 0.10	0	$0.00
Implied share value					**$8.40**

The earnings of $1 per share in this case were less than "perfect" because some components of earnings were not sustainable. The lower quality of earnings resulted in a stock price of $8.40 rather than $12.00.

RESEARCH ON QUALITY OF EARNINGS AND STOCK PRICES

As early as 1972, Beaver and Dukes discovered that the stock market was efficient in that it valued net income amounts differently based on differences in the perceived value of the earnings reported. They found that P/E ratios used by the stock market differentiated systematically among firms based on the method of depreciation used. Firms that used straight-line depreciation tended to have lower P/E ratios than firms using accelerated depreciation. Straight-line depreciation would, of course, result in higher net income than accelerated depreciation. This early research can be interpreted as evidence that one factor affecting quality of earnings was linked to stock price.[12]

A continuing research question is: "Are other factors affecting quality of earnings linked to stock prices?" Lev and Thiagarajan report that:

> *"For the 1980's, the fundamentals add approximately 70 percent, on average, to the explanatory power of earnings with respect to excess returns. . . . We hypothesize that the fundamental signals identified in this study are used by investors to assess the persistence (sometimes referred to as 'quality') and growth of reported earnings."*[13]

For them the answer to the question is: "Yes, factors affecting quality of earnings are linked to stock prices."

---

[12] Beaver, W., and R. Dukes. "Interperiod Tax Allocation, Earnings Expectations and the Behavior of Security Prices." *Accounting Review,* 47 (1972): 320-332.

[13] Lev, B., and S. R. Thiagarajan. "Fundamental Information Analysis." *Journal of Accounting Research,* 31 (1993): 190-191.

Since quality-of-earnings factors are linked to stock prices, the next question for study is: "Do stock prices fully reflect quality of earnings information?" This is harder to answer because there are so many different factors that affect quality of earnings. Logic would suggest that probably not all of them are fully reflected in stock prices due to both the limitations of human ability to process information and the fact that, as numerous studies have shown, the stock market is not 100 percent efficient.

This view is supported by research that examined annual financial statement data for 40,679 firm years (data on a single firm for a 10-year period equals 10 firm years) for the period 1962 to 1991. This study found that "stock prices are found to act as if investors 'fixate' on earnings, failing to reflect fully information contained in the accrual and cash flow components of current earnings until that information impacts future earnings."[14] The bottom line is that the stock market partially, but not fully, adjusts for quality-of-earnings-related information.

The message for readers, then, is that executives can favorably affect their company's stock price by employing the earnings management techniques discussed in this book even though quality of earnings is a factor considered by the stock market.

What is the penalty for very low-quality earnings? "Very low quality earnings" may be considered synonymous with earnings that have been managed to an excessive degree. Several studies have found that the capital markets impose substantial costs on firms believed to have engaged in excessive earnings management or earnings manipulation. It is estimated that the average stock price drop is 9 percent when earnings manipulations are alleged by a credible source like the SEC.[15]

CASE STUDY: QWEST COMMUNICATIONS

One company that has generated controversy due to allegedly overly aggressive accounting practices is the telecom Qwest Communications International Inc. Qwest's controversy was sparked by the following accounting issues:

- Qwest in 2001 at first insisted on carrying an investment in KPNQwest, a European telecom network, at more than $7 billion even though its market value was lower. Qwest wrote the investment down to $1.3 billion later in the year when this became a public issue.
- The company boosted the assumed return on its pension plan assets from 8.8 percent to 9.4 percent. This change in assumptions resulted in pension plan income.

---

[14] Sloan, R. G. "Do Stock Prices Fully Reflect Information In Accruals and Cash Flows About Future Earnings?" *Accounting Review,* 71 (1996): 289.

[15] Dechow, P. M., R. G. Sloan, and A. P. Sweeney. "Causes and Consequences of Earnings Manipulation: An Analysis of Firms Subject to Enforcement Actions by the SEC." *Contemporary Accounting Research,* 13 (1996): 3.

- Qwest also used several other accounting practices that were questioned by analysts. The basic problem was that the accounting practices "while legal, were so aggressive that it would be difficult for Qwest to hit future revenue and profit growth targets."[16]
- The company also ran into difficulty when it proposed to book $300 million in general revenue for buying and selling telecom gear to a small startup called Calpoint LLC. Calpoint was developing communications services based on new optical technology that Qwest proposed to market to its own customers. Analysts were dubious about this revenue classification because selling telecom equipment "is hardly Qwest's business."[17] Analysts were concerned that this classification of revenue would confuse true gross and net margins for the company. After criticism, Qwest agreed to break these revenues out separately.

Qwest's stock dropped from approximately $40 a share on January 2, 2001 to $17 a share on September 27, 2001. Though much of the decline was related to a decline in the market generally and in the telecom industry in particular, "based on price-to-cash flow ratios, there is a 10 percent to 20 percent discount relative to other Bells, largely because of concerns over accounting issues."[18] Figure 7.3 (page 100) displays Qwest's share price changes.

This case illustrates the problems that can arise from concerns over quality of earnings. The stock market will penalize a company's share price if there are concerns over quality of earnings. Qwest Communication's share price appears to have declined during 2001 due to analysts' concerns over the company's GAAP choices and quality of earnings.

---

[16] Elstrom, P. "On The Firing Line At Qwest—It's Two Morgan Stanley Analysts versus the Telecom in an Unusual Feud Over Accounting." *Business Week,* October 29, 2001, p. 72.

[17] Ibid., p. 77.

[18] Ibid., p. 73.

Figure 7.3. Changes in Qwest Share Prices During 2001[19]

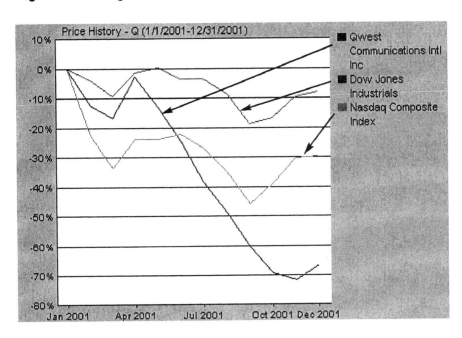

8 MANAGING EARNINGS AND ANALYST EXPECTATIONS

This chapter explains how to implement a long-term earnings management plan. It also discusses how analysts' expectations of future earnings enter into the process and how those expectations can be influenced.

Good ideas are easy to come by but getting them implemented can be much harder. Fortunately, earnings may be managed using the following steps:

1. Forecast the future earnings stream.
2. Evaluate economic factors likely to affect the earnings stream.
3. Select earnings management methods that will improve the earnings stream.

Many executives will delegate these steps to their accounting and finance professionals. Others will be more actively involved. Regardless of their degree of involvement, however, all executives will benefit from understanding how to implement an earnings management plan.

FORECAST THE FUTURE EARNINGS STREAM

The first step is to make a forecast of what future earnings are likely to be. The forecast is necessary so you can decide whether it is desirable to manage earnings up or down during a particular fiscal period—do not assume that you will always want to manage earnings in an upward direction. What needs to be done is to determine what a sustainable level of earnings is and manage earnings in that direction, whether it is up or down.

Many companies have internal forecasting systems that produce fairly reliable data, but others do not. It makes sense to use the internal system if it produces reliable, timely estimates.

Public companies normally release quarterly earnings data so it is usually best to forecast earnings quarterly. That lets you link your forecasts to the publicly dis-closed quarterly earnings estimates that analysts use.

Remember that the future has not happened yet; it is not known to anyone. The best anyone can do is to use relationships from the past and try to make educated guesses about possible changes and what the future may hold.

TYPES OF FORECASTING

The forecasting process can be extremely complex or relatively simple, depending on how much detail is included. Companies with multiple business units in differ-ent industries will want a separate forecast for each business unit, which will then be aggregated into an overall company forecast.

One type of forecasting is *structural modeling,* which attempts to predict one variable using a second variable that is thought to cause changes in the first vari-able. For example, advertising expense may be used to try to predict sales revenue if its influence on sales has been demonstrated previously.

In structural modeling, since a single variable rarely completely controls another variable, numerous factors have to be analyzed to see if they cause a change in the variable being forecast. Given how difficult it is to determine which variables cause others to change, these models can be very complex. They can also incorporate a large number of variables into complex equations.

Time-series modeling simply applies a model that matches how a variable, such as net income, changes through time. The basic assumption in using this type of model is that the past will continue into the future without significant change.

Exponential Smoothing Forecasting Example

A simple example will be used to illustrate the time-series modeling process. Assume that you are interested in forecasting next quarter's net income for Company A. The quarterly net income as publicly reported for the last 4 years is listed in Table 8.1.

The trend shown is this table is demonstrated more clearly in Figure 8.1.

Although there are numerous methods of time-series forecasting, for simplic-ity we will first use the exponential smoothing method, which is built into many electronic spreadsheets. The basic assumption behind this method is that the lagged average trend from the past will continue into the future. Each new forecast is composed of a percentage of the actual value from the previous period and a per-centage of the forecast value from the previous period, with the two summing to 100 percent. The relative weighting between the actual and the forecast values depends on how much weight you think should be placed on the actual results from the period. Figure 8.2 displays the exponential smoothing results for the previous data.

As you can see from the figure, the high and low points in the net income series are smoothed out by the exponential smoothing fitted line.

Table 8.1.Time-Series Modeling Example

	Year 1				Year 2				Year 3				Year 4				Year 5
	Q1	*Q2*	*Q3*	*Q4*	*Q1*	*Q2*	*Q3*	*Q4*	*Q1*	*Q2*	*Q3*	*Q4*	*Q1*	*Q2*	*Q3*	*Q4*	*Q1*
Net income	1,050	1,123	1,143	1,220	1,179	1,140	1,103	1,178	1,139	1,273	1,420	1,582	1,602	1,542	1,485	1,653	???

Figure 8.1. Company A: Net Income Growth

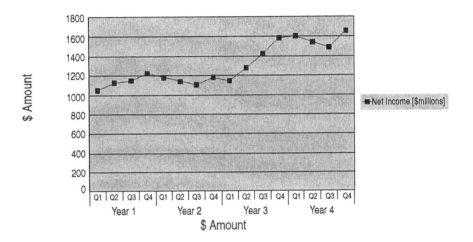

The formula for this model is:

70 percent of prior period actual net income + 30 percent of prior period forecast
= Forecasted amount.

We can use this formula to make an earnings forecast for the previous data. The forecast formula is:

70 percent x $1,653 + 30 percent x $1,491 = $1,605.

The forecast net income for the first quarter of Year 5 for Company A is thus $1,605.[1] This forecast is indicated in Figure 8.2 by the last data point, which extends the forecast line to Year 5-Quarter 1.

---

[1] $1,653 is the net income indicated in Year 4-Quarter 4 of the preceding table. $1,491 is the amount forecast for Year 4-Quarter 4, which could have been read directly from Figure 8.2 if the data values had been printed. The data values were omitted to keep the figure from getting too cluttered to read.

Figure 8.2. Exponential Smoothing

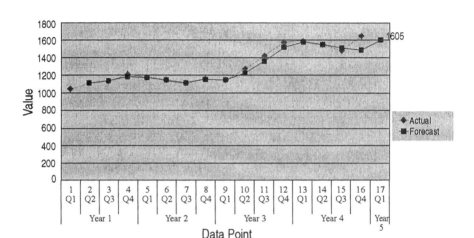

Data Point

Simple Regression Forecasting Example

Another common time-series forecasting method is simple regression analysis. This method simply fits a straight line to the data points that can then be extended into future periods to make a forecast for those periods. This method, too, is built into most electronic spreadsheets. Figure 8.3 shows a regression model fitted to the Company A data.

The line fits the data fairly well so it is appropriate to use this model to project net income into the next quarter.[2] The line has been extended to Year 5-Quarter 1. The value of the data point indicated by the end of the line is a forecasted net income of $1,630.

At this point two different time series forecasting methods have produced two different forecasts: Exponential smoothing forecast $1,605 while the simple regression forecast $1,630. Which one should be used? The answer to this question is discussed next.

EVALUATE ECONOMIC FACTORS

Since there are numerous forecasting methods, each based on different assumptions, there could be several different earnings forecasts. The multiplicity of forecast estimates can easily be seen by looking at the dispersion of analysts' forecasts for any public company. Table 8.2 shows analysts' earnings forecasts for Microsoft as of December 21, 2001.

---

[2] The statistical measure of fit for this line is its adjusted R^2. The measure can vary from 0 to 1, with 1 indicating a perfect fit. The actual adjusted R^2 for this line was 0.78, which is fairly good.

Figure 8.3. Company A: Simple Regression

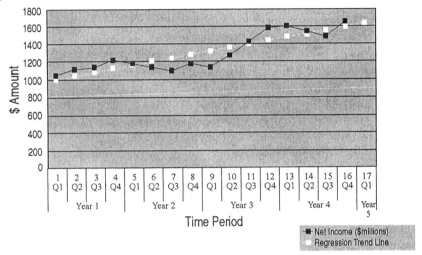

Table 8.2. Estimates of Microsoft Corporation Earnings[3]

Earnings Estimates	Qtr (12/01)	Qtr (3/02)	FY (6/02)	FY (6/03)
Average estimate	0.47	0.46	1.81	2.07
Number of analysts	25	25	28	19
High estimate	0.52	0.53	1.95	2.23
Low estimate	0.41	0.42	1.60	1.85
Year-ago earnings per share	0.47	0.44	1.81	1.81
Growth rate	0.85%	3.45%	0.02%	14.28%

The table shows that earnings forecasts ranged from $0.42 to $0.53 per share for the quarter ending March 2002—an approximately 25 percent variation. The analysts obviously used different assumptions and forecasting methods.

Executives have to use their own knowledge of the company and the economic factors surrounding it to evaluate individual forecasts. Knowledge of the assumptions behind the modeling method also helps.

EVALUATING THE EXPONENTIAL SMOOTHING FORECAST

The exponential smoothing model forecast $1,605 net income for Year 5-Quarter 1. From Figure 8.2 we can see that the exponential smoothing model was fairly close to the actual net income amount for all time periods except Year 4-Quarter 4,

[3] *http://moneycentral.msn.com/investor/invsub/analyst/earnest.asp?Page=Earnings Estimates&Symbol=msft.* Earnings estimates data provided by Zacks Investment Research. accessed December 21, 2001.

the last period displayed. We would have a great deal more confidence in the model's forecast if this difference had not occurred.

Exponential smoothing models basically incorporate only the actual data for the last three time periods. Thus, for our example, each forecast effectively ignores actual data before the last three quarters. This type of model is therefore most appropriate when only the most recent past is significant.

Figure 8.2 shows that for Year 4-Quarters 1, 2, and 3, net income was trending down before it sharply reversed upward for Year 4-Quarter 4. In making the Year 4-Quarter 4 forecast, the model gave a 30 percent weight to the Year 4-Quarter 3 forecast, which was low. This failure to react to a sudden change is typical of exponential smoothing models.

Executives may or may not know that the exponential smoothing model usually lags changes but they should know what caused net income to spike sharply upward in Year 4-Quarter 4. This knowledge will let them evaluate whether the net income increase is sustainable into the following year. If it is, the $1,605 forecast may be too low.

EVALUATING THE SIMPLE REGRESSION FORECAST

The simple regression model forecast $1,630 in earnings. This model reflects the trend for the past 16 quarters. It does not ignore any prior data. Executives should be able to use their knowledge of the company to figure out why actual earnings were below this trend for Year 2-Quarters 2, 3, and 4 and above it for Year 3-Quarter 4 and Year 4-Quarter 1. Once the reasons are determined, an executive should then be able to determine if these reasons make it likely that the company will achieve a net income of $1,630 consistent with its four-year trend.

If the executive does not think that the past 20 quarters are totally relevant, it is possible to run the regression model on a smaller portion of the data. For example, as Figure 8.4 shows, if the model were run on only the data for Year 4-Quarters 1, 2, 3, and 4, the model's net income prediction would be $1,595. This difference occurs because the time-series trend has been calculated for only the last four quarters, not the last 20.

In summary, executives should use their knowledge of the company and the assumptions behind the forecasting method to evaluate forecasts.

SELECT EARNINGS MANAGEMENT METHODS

Once you have a forecast for a future period, you can evaluate whether it would be desirable to manage earnings in an up or down direction. As you may recall, earnings goals are met in the following order:

1. Avoid losses.
2. Report increases in quarterly earnings.
3. Meet analysts' earnings forecasts.

Figure 8.4. Company A: Simple Regression Projection Using Only Year 4 Data

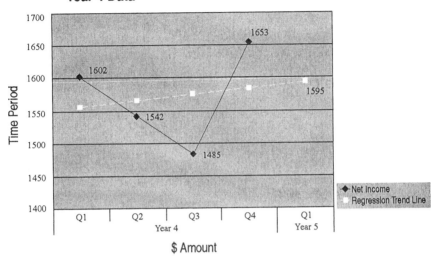

$ Amount

Assume you have determined that the regression forecast of $1,630 is the best forecast for Year 5-Quarter 1. This will correspond to a decline from the $1,653 earned for Year 4-Quarter 4. Since you are not facing a loss situation, you can move to meet goal 2, reporting an increase in quarterly earnings. This suggests that, if possible, earnings need to be managed upward for the next quarter, so you look for an earnings management technique that can accomplish this. Appendix A: Earnings Management Evaluation Checklist can help jog your memory about possible techniques.

Once you have identified possible techniques, you must evaluate their potential effect on future quarters. This evaluation can take place using a matrix like the one shown in Table 8.3.

Table 8.3. Evaluation Matrix for Earnings Management Techniques

	Amount of Increased Earnings							
	Qtr 1	Qtr 2	Qtr 3	Qtr 4	Qtr 5	Qtr 6	Qtr 7	Qtr 8
Projected earnings	$1,630	$1,680	$1,740	$1,750	$1,800	$1,850	$1,910	$1,920
1. Switch to straight-line depreciation	10	10	10	10	5	5	5	5
2. Revise pension expense estimate	20	20	20	20	30	30	30	30
3. Estimate warranty costs	15	15	15	15	-5	-5	-5	-5
Managed earnings	$1,675	$1,725	$1,785	$1,795	$1,830	$1,880	$1,940	$1,950

As you can see from Table 8.2, the earnings effect can vary by quarter and can switch from positive to negative, or vice versa, depending on the technique employed.

MANAGING ANALYSTS' EXPECTATIONS

The stock of most public companies is followed by a wide variety of analysts, who can have a strong influence on the stock price. Typically, the larger the company, the more analysts who follow the stock. In Table 8.1, Microsoft had from 19 to 28 analysts making earnings projections. Smart managers manage analysts' expectations, a process that is sometimes referred to as providing guidance:

> *"Guidance involves interaction between a company spokesman and the analysts who follow the firm. The spokesman will give a set of vague projections to assist analysts in creating next quarter's projections without divulging what is happening inside the firm. For example, a spokesman may suggest that in the next quarter the firm's revenue will be higher or lower, that expenses may be increasing or decreasing, or that taxes may be changing. Guidance has become a primary line of communication between firms and their analysts.*
>
> *Because the firm's information is disseminated through the market without giving an individual or single entity an advantage, investors are viewed as playing on a level field and the number of lawsuits and SEC interference is minimized. Guidance also fosters uniformity for the analysts' estimates, which helps keep the consensus where the firm wants it."[4]*

Analysts use so many valuation models and investment strategies that it is impossible to know what they all are. However, we do know that many of the models value future earnings and place a premium on earnings that increase steadily. Smart executives can package their earnings to meet analysts' expectations by undertaking the following activities:

- **Release their own achievable earnings forecasts.** Earnings forecasts should come from a reliable internal system that produces reasonably accurate forecasts. If analysts believe company forecasts are reliable, they will use them as the basis for making their own earnings forecasts, or will at a minimum use them as a comparison for their own. This should reduce variation in analysts' earnings forecasts, which can lead to a more stable stock price.

- **Leave a little slack in the company forecast.** This leaves the company a cushion to fall back upon so that even if economic events are not as favorable as was expected, the company can still achieve the forecast. It is better to come in a few cents a share above the consensus analysts' earnings forecast than a few cents under; price reactions to bad news tend to be stronger than reactions to good news.

---

[4] Ferraro, S., and C. McPeak. "Managing Earnings or Cooking the Books?" *Graziadio Business Report*. http://gbr.pepperdine.edu/003/reporting.html. Accessed December 26, 2001.

- *Promptly release additional information if events change.* Analysts often pick up quickly on company or industry-wide earnings problems. Lack of current information may lead them to assume a worst-case scenario, which in turn may cause an excessive or unnecessary market price reaction. Timely, relevant information permits analysts to adjust their forecasts appropriately, leading to a more appropriate market price reaction. This open also helps a company build a reputation for honest information policies, and a good reputation can reduce the perceived risk in earnings estimates and thereby help the stock price.
- *Retain some operational and accounting earnings management flexibility.* It is best keep some earnings management techniques in reserve. Economic events are somewhat unpredictable. When something unexpected happens, having a technique in reserve techniques will give you a better chance of meeting your earnings goals.

CHANGING THE CAPITAL MARKETS

Only ethical earnings management that is within the bounds of GAAP will result in better capital markets.

Individuals who believe that earnings management, in any form, is a negative factor in the capital markets should work to change the institutional and regulatory environment that currently permits and encourages earnings management.

9 COOKIE JAR RESERVE TECHNIQUES

This chapter discusses and illustrates popular cookie jar reserve techniques for earnings management.

Perhaps the most widely employed earnings management techniques are "cookie jar reserves." The reason is simple. As the name implies, these techniques permit management to store various amounts until a time when there are pressures on income. When the rainy day comes, management just reaches into the cookie jar and extracts as much of an income boost or decrease as is needed.

HOW COOKIE JAR RESERVES WORK

A normal feature of GAAP-based accrual accounting is that management must estimate and record an expense for obligations that must be paid in the future as a result of events in the current fiscal year. Since what will happen is not known with certainty, there is often substantial uncertainty in the estimation process. Instead of one right answer there is a range of reasonably possible answers. Because management is forced by GAAP to select a single estimate from within this range, there is an opportunity for earnings management.

When management selects estimates from the high end of the range of reasonably possible expenses, the effect is to record more expense in the current fiscal period than would be recorded if a lower estimate had been selected. This may make it possible to record less expense in a future fiscal period. Management created a cookie jar reserve (this can also be called "financial slack") that can be tapped to get an earnings boost in the future.

BAD DEBTS AND COOKIE JAR RESERVES

To illustrate, we can look at a common expense estimation, the bad debt expense for receivables. A company recording bad debt expense makes entries like the following:

Increase income statement account →→ Bad debt expense
Increase balance sheet account ——→ Allowance for uncollectible accounts

The effect of the first entry is to write off part of an asset balance as an expense. The allowance for uncollectible accounts on the balance sheet is subtracted from the book value of receivables to reduce the net balance to the estimated realizable value.

Assume that, for Year 1, a company has a pretax profit of $4 million with bad debt expense of $2.5 million included in the computation. This income amount is believed to be above the long-term sustainable income level, so the company wants to "save" some of it for the future. Normal procedures produce an estimated bad debt expense for Year 1 that ranges from $2 million to $3 million with $2.5 million being the most likely estimate. If management selects $3 million as the current period bad debt expense, the effect is to create a $0.5 million cookie jar reserve.

Whether the reserve is real or not depends on whether actual bad debts related to Year 1 are kept equal to or less than $2.5 million. This cannot normally be known with certainty until Year 2, when the accounts actually prove to be uncollectible. If net pre-tax income in Year 2 declines to $3.1 million and actual uncollectible accounts for Year 1 and Year 2 are each $2.5 million, then Year 2 does get a $0.5 million income boost (see Table 9.1).

Table 9.1. Cookie Jar Reserve Effects

Item	Year 1	Year 2
Income before cookie jar reserve	$4,000,000	$3,100,000
Less cookie jar reserve effect of increasing allowance for uncollectible accounts to $ 3 million in Year 1 and allowing it to fall to $2 .5 million in Year 2	-500,000	+500,000
Income after effect of cookie jar reserve	$3,500,000	$3,600,000

This income boost in Year 2 occurs because in Year 2 it will only be necessary to record $2 million in bad debts expense because $0.5 is carried over from the previous year in the allowance for doubtful accounts. The journal entry for Year 2 would be as follows:

Increase income statement account ——→ Bad debt expense $2,000,000
Increase balance sheet account →→ Allowance for doubtful accounts $2,000,000

If expenses in the second year actually turn out to be at the high end of the estimation range at $3 million, the cookie jar will be empty because the allowance for doubtful accounts created in Year 1 would be wiped out. There will then be no earnings boost.

The example lowered net income in Year 1 through creation of the reserve. It would also have been possible to increase net income in Year 1 by recording the bad debt expense as $2 million, the lower end of the estimation range.

RESEARCH ON MANAGING EARNINGS WITH BAD DEBTS

McNichols and Wilson examined the bad debt accruals for 2,038 firm-year observations over the period 1967-1985 to determine whether managers manipulate earnings. The 116 firms in their sample were selected from the three industries (publishing, business services, and nondurable wholesales) with the highest median ratios of receivables to total assets and allowance for bad debts to income.

The median ratio of bad debt write-offs to sales for the firms in the sample was 0.30 percent. Although this is relatively small, the average bad debts provision was 20 percent of income. The authors concluded:

> *"Our results support the hypothesis that the discretionary component of the provision for bad debts is income-decreasing for firms whose earnings are unusually high or low."*[1]

This means they found that the bad debts expense estimation process is used to manage earnings. Firms that were expecting unusually high earnings used this estimation to lower those earnings. Firms that were expecting a bad year used it to lower earnings even further.

SPECIFIC COOKIE JAR RESERVE ACCOUNTS

Accounts other than bad debt write-offs where cookie jar reserves are commonly created include:

- Sales return allowances.
- Inventory write-downs.
- Warranty costs.
- Pension expenses.
- Pension plan termination.
- Percentage of completion for long-term contracts.

The following sections briefly explain both the GAAP requirements and how the cookie jar reserve process works for each of these accounts.

---

[1] McNicholsand, M., and G. P. Wilson. "Evidence of Earnings Management from the Provision for Bad Debts." *Journal of Accounting Research,* 26, Supplement (1988): 3.

SALES RETURNS AND ALLOWANCES

GAAP requires that receivables be recorded in the balance sheet at *net realizable value*. This is the amount of cash that is ultimately expected to be collected from the receivables. That means that any factors affecting collectibility of receivables should be taken into account. One such factor is sales returns and allowances.

Sales that are expected to be returned for credit or have some adjustment made to the selling price are recorded in sales returns and allowances. A company expecting $5 million of sales returns and allowances during Year 2 for sales made during Year 1 would record the following entry in Year 1:

Increase income statement account →Sales returns and allowances $5 million

Increase balance sheet account →Allowance for sales returns and allowances $5 million

Since the returns and allowances amount is usually estimated, rather than known with certainty, it provides an opportunity for earnings management.

INVENTORY WRITE-DOWNS

GAAP requires that inventories be written down from historical cost—the purchase price or cost to manufacture—to net realizable value when there is a significant decline in the utility (value)of the inventory. Such a decline may occur for reasons such as:

- Inventory obsolescence.
- Damaged goods.
- Price changes.

The entry to record the write-down in inventory would appear as follows:

Increase income statement account → Cost of goods sold (or Loss due to market decline)

Decrease balance sheet account ⟶ Inventory

In some cases, companies may choose to use a contra-inventory account called Allowance to Reduce Inventory to Market" rather than reducing the inventory account directly. This account works like the allowance accounts associated with receivables.

Determining the value of the inventory may require complex estimation procedures that provide an opportunity for earnings management.

WARRANTY COSTS

Many companies that sell products provide warranties—product guarantees—for them that are included in the price of the product. Claims made by customers under warranty provisions constitute a business expense that reduces net income.

Companies having material warranty expenses or warranties that cover relatively long periods are required by GAAP to use the accrual basis for recording warranties. Under this method, warranty cost for items sold in Year 1 must be estimated recorded as an expense in Year 1, even though warranty claims may not be made by customers until a future year.

The entry to record $10 million of estimated product warranty costs to be incurred in future years would be:

Increase income statement account ➤ Warranty expense $10 million

Increase balance sheet account ➤ Estimated liability under warranties $10 million

Determining future warranty costs for sales made during the current fiscal year can be a complex estimation procedure that provides an opportunity for earnings management.

PENSION EXPENSE

Pension expense for defined benefit plans is for many companies the most difficult expense account to estimate. The difficulties stem from both the nature of pension costs and the detailed GAAPrequirements for pension accounting. GAAPbasically requires that pension expense be recorded on an accrual basis based on estimated future pension costs. The entry to record this for most companies would be similar to the following:

Increase income statement account ➤ Pension expense

Increase balance sheet account ➤ Pension liability

The pension liability would then be reduced by contributions made by the company into the pension plan. Once the plan is fully funded, the liability would be reduced to zero.

Figure 9.1 illustrates the basic pension expense problem.

Figure 9.1. Pension Expense

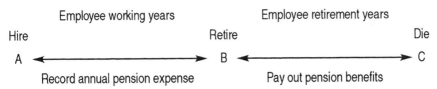

Companies must record annual pension expense during an employee's working years by estimating the present value of pension benefits to be paid out during the employee's retirement years. For companies with a large workforce, this is a very complex estimation process.

The time span for the A to B segment, employee working years, may range from 1 year to 40 or more. The time span for the B to C segment, employee retirement years, may range from 1 year to 30 or more. Thus, in order to properly record pension expense, management may have to estimate a payout that may happen as much as 70 years in the future!

Among the other components of pensions that must be estimated are:

- Expected return on plan assets.
- Discount rate.
- Rate of compensation increase expected for workforce.
- Average service life of covered employees.

Small changes in these estimations can have a big effect on current year pension expense. In fact, David Henry reported in *Business Week* that during 2001 pension plan expenses lifted the earnings of the Standard & Poor's 500 stock index by 2 percent:

> *"It was an amazing feat since plan assets dropped 5 percent and liabilities rose 8 percent at the same time. The imaginary income was based on self-serving estimates and remnants of paper gains on equity investments logged during the bull market."[2]*

One can only conclude that many managers in the Fortune 500 companies are taking advantage of the earnings management opportunities available in the pension area.

PENSION PLAN TERMINATION

A pension plan may be viewed as a giant piggy bank. When investments in the pension plan earn more than expected, the piggy bank holds more money than is required to pay future pension obligations. If the excess is large enough, a company may decide to terminate the plan and record a gain in the income statement for the excess. GAAP requires that such a gain be recognized over a period at least 10 years.[3] There may also be substantial taxes due on the gains.

To crack the pension piggy bank and terminate the plan, a company must pay pension participants what is owed them. This is often done by buying annuities for pension claimants.

To illustrate, assume that a company pension plan has $500 million in assets. For $300 million it can buy annuity contracts that will fully pay pension participants. Since the plan asset value exceeds the cost of settling the pension liabilities, the company can record a $200 million gain before tax, amortized as a $20 million gain each year for 10 years starting with the year of termination.

---

[2] Henry, D. "Cleaning up the Numbers." *Business Week* Online, March 24, 2003. *http://www.businessweek.com/bw50/content/mar2003/a3826040.htm*. Accessed December 7, 2003.

[3] "Employers' Accounting for Settlements and Curtailments of Defined Benefit Pension Plans and for Termination Benefits." FASB Statement No. 88. Stamford, CT: FASB 1985; *http://www.pwccomperio.com/search97cgi/s97is_english.dll/search97cgi/inetsrch_eng -lish.ini?action=formgen&Template=comperio.hts*. Accessed December 30, 2001.

Cash-Balance Pension Plans

An increasingly popular type of pension plan is a cash-balance pension plan. Arcady and Mellors reported in the *Journal of Accountancy* that:

> *". . . an estimated 16 percent of Fortune 100 companies have switched to a so-called cash balance formula."*[4]

This type of plan allows employees to transfer pension benefits when they change employers or retire. The transfer is accomplished by paying the employees a lump sum (the cash balance) at that time. The employee can then roll over the lump-sum payment into a self-directed individual retirement account (IRA) or another qualified plan.

Companies that convert a traditional defined benefit pension plan to a cash-balance pension plan may be able to record a reduction in their annual pension expense similar to what would be recorded by actually terminating the plan.[5]

PERCENTAGE OF COMPLETION FOR LONG-TERM CONTRACTS

Two possible methods of revenue and expense recognition for companies earning revenue under long-term contracts are:

- Completed contract method.
- Percentage-of-completion method.

These methods would typically be used in industries like construction, ship-building, and software development.

Under the completed contract method a company waits until a contract is completed and then records all revenue and expenses from the contract. With the percentage-of-completion method income is recorded as earned over the life of the contract.

Because the percentage-of-completion method is preferred under GAAP—it is presumed to do a better job of matching expenses with related revenue to get a more meaningful net income—normally that would be the method of choice. GAAP, however, permits a company to use the completed contract method if meaningful estimates of degree of completion cannot be made.

Under the percentage-of-completion method, at its fiscal year-end a company estimates the percentage of work done during the year under the contract. The company then recognizes that percentage of total revenue expected and deducts costs incurred to date to compute net income for the period under the contract.

---

[4] Arcady, A. T., and F. Mellors. "Cash-Balance Conversions." *Journal of Accountancy,* February, 2000, p. 22. *http://www.AICPA.org/pubs/jofa/feb2000/arcady.htm.* Accessed October 18, 2001.
[5] Ibid., 22-28.

Assume ABC Company is engaged in a two-year, $10 million contract to write software for another company. At the end of the first year, ABC estimates it has completed 40 percent of the contract and costs incurred to date total $3.8 million. ABC Company's income statement for the contract would appear as follows:

Revenue earned (40 percent x $10 million)	$4,000,000
Expenses	3,800,000
Income from contract	$ 200,000

Determining the percentage of completion for work under a contract may require exercise of considerable judgment in many situations. For the software example, percentage of completion could be based on any of the following metrics, and these metrics might produce conflicting results:

- Lines of computer code written in relation to total lines expected.
- Number of staff-hours incurred in relation to total hours expected.
- Degree of reliability/failure testing completed.
- Contract milestones.

Even if only a single metric were used, it might be difficult to get a reliable estimate for that metric. Typically, some judgment is needed in estimating the percentage of completion, which provides an opportunity for earnings management.

10 BIG BATH TECHNIQUES

This chapter discusses and illustrates popular Big Bath *techniques for earnings management.*

There is a saying, "If you have to stick your toe in cold water, you might as well jump in for a big bath," that nicely sums up another popular method of earnings management. As we have mentioned several times, the Number One earnings goal is to avoid losses. Nevertheless, when a loss must be reported, it often makes sense to report as big a loss as is reasonably possible. This puts all the bad news related to earnings in the current period and clears the decks for good earnings-related news in future periods.

It is not uncommon to see big baths when there is a change in management. They allow the new management to attribute all responsibility for the big losses to the previous management.

HOW THE BIG BATH TECHNIQUE WORKS

Under this approach, when a bad earnings result is expected, a firm takes additional loss write-offs that make the financial results even worse for the current fiscal period. That means the company will not have to face the big costs later on. Suppose a firm expects a $100 million loss in the current fiscal year because overcapacity will force it to close one manufacturing plant. The company also thinks the economy may soften further and possibly force additional layoffs and plant closings that will cost an additional $150 million in the next fiscal year. If it decides to take a big bath approach, it would record a $250 million loss in the current fiscal year so that it can report a profit in the following plan. To do that, of course, the company will have to formulate a restructuring plan that incorporates actions ultimately expected to cost $250 million.

Big bath write-offs affect the timing of expense recognition but not the amount. Big bath losses are usually incurred in one of the following categories:

- Operations restructuring.
- Asset impairment.
- Troubled debt restructuring.
- Discontinued operations.

CASE STUDY: SCOTT PAPER—PART A-RESTRUCTURING

Scott Paper Company is an old-line company founded in Philadelphia in 1879. It was the first to market rolls of tissue for toilet paper and paper towels for the home. By 1990, its sales had grown to $5.4 billion in 20 countries, but then competition and some poor diversification choices caused it to lose market share for four years in a row.[1] The company tried a number of divestiture and restructuring activities between 1990 and 1993 to try to turn things around but these were not considered totally successful.

"Chainsaw" Al Dunlap was hired as CEO in April 1994 with a charge to definitely turn the company around. He implemented a major cost-cutting and restructuring plan that resulted in 11,000 employees losing their jobs. "Under his leadership, Scott's stock rose 225 percent, adding $6.3 billion in value to the company."[2] Scott Paper Company later completed a $9.4 billion merger with Kimberly-Clark Corporation.

Scott Paper Company had created a restructuring reserve before hiring Dunlap. The 1993 charge against net income of $489.6 million helped to reduce the income to a $277 million net loss. In other words, the 1993 big bath not only wiped out the income for the year, it created a reportable loss.

During 1994, Dunlap's first year with the company, Scott Paper Company was able to write off $530 million of expenses against the restructuring reserve that had been created in prior years. This meant the company reported a 1994 net income of $209.8 million despite continued massive restructuring and the huge expense write-off. Footnote 3 from the December 31, 1994 financial statements of Scott Paper Company details the restructuring charges (see Figure 10.1).

[1] "The Paper Shredder." *http://bsstrategist.com/00jun27/2story.htm.* Accessed November 7, 2001.
[2] Byrne, J. A., and J. Weber. "The Shredder." *Business Week* Online. *http://www.business-week.com/ 1996/03/b34581.htm.* Accessed November 14, 2001.

**Figure 10.1. Scott Paper Company: December 31, 1994
Financial Statement, Footnote 3**

3. Restructuring

In 1993, the Company recorded a charge for its
planned restructuring and productivity improvement pro-
grams. The plan included the estimated costs to further
reduce its work force as well as the costs to realign
and shut down some older and inefficient assets. The
1993 charge of $489.6 million was combined with the
balance from previous restructuring plans of $149.4
million. Included in the 1993 charge was $88.5 million
for S. D. Warren.

In August 1994, this plan was modified to accelerate the timing and increase the total of the work
force reductions. This expanded plan was completed by
year end 1994 and no additional charges were needed
to achieve the restructuring. The major elements of
the 1994 plan were:

(Millions)	Charges Against Reserve	Reserve December 31, 1994
Cost of work force reductions	$330.1	$83.8
Plant rationalization	107.7	11.8
Divested businesses	78.5	11.9
Other	14.1	1.1
	$530.4	$108.6[3]

The bottom line (literally) is that the big bath in the previous year allowed
Scott Paper Company to report net income in 1994, despite the massive restructuring. This financial performance later helped them negotiate the $9.4 billion
merger with Kimberly-Clark Corporation.

PART B—BIG BATH REPORTING

The Scott Paper Company income statement for 1993 and 1994 is presented in
Figure 10.2. It provides a good example of how two of the big bath techniques
might be reported.

---

[3] Scott Paper Company 10-K for Fiscal Year Ending December 31, 1994. *http://www.sec.
gov/Archives/edgar/data/87949/0000950109-95-000987.txt*. Accessed November 7, 2001.

Note first that the 1993 restructuring charge of $401.1 million was taken as part of regular costs and expenses, so it reduced regular operating income (income from continuing operations). Then note that the 1993 loss of $51.3 million due to discontinued operations is reported at the bottom of the income statement *after* regular operating income.

Figure 10.2. Scott Paper Company Income Statements for 1993 and 1994

Consolidated Operations

Scott Paper Company

(In millions)	1994	1993
Sales	$3,581.1	3,584.9
Costs and expenses		
Product costs	2,510.8	2,576.4
Marketing and distribution	479.9	536.7
Research, administration and general	189.0	208.3
Restructuring and divestments	--	**401.1**
Other	(100.2)	8.5
	3,079.5	3,731.0
Income (loss) from continuing operations	501.6	(146.1)
Interest expense	131.2	123.8
Other income and (expense)	9.6	4.1
Income (loss) from continuing operations before taxes	380.0	(265.8)
Income taxes	139.8	(49.7)
Income (loss) from continuing operations before share of earnings (loss) of international equity affiliates, extraordinary loss and cumulative effect of accounting change	240.2	(216.1)
Share of earnings (loss) of international equity affiliates	23.9	(21.7)

Figure 10.2. Scott Paper Company Income Statements for 1993 and 1994, *Cont'd*

```
Income (loss) from continuing
  operations before extraordinary
  loss and cumulative effect of
  accounting change                       264.1   (237.8)
```

Discontinued operation--printing
**   and publishing papers:**
** Income (loss) from operations through**
**   December 20, 1994,net of income**
**   tax expense (benefit) of $4.0,**
**   and $(14.3)for 1994, and 1993**
**   respectively   6.8   (51.3)**
** Gain (loss) on disposal   --   --**

```
Income (loss) before extraordinary
  loss and cumulative effect of
  accounting change                       270.9   (289.1)
Extraordinary loss on early
  extinguishment of debt, net of
  income tax benefit of $35.8 and
  $5.2 for 1994 and 1993, respectively  (61.1)    (9.6)
Cumulative effect of change in
  accounting for income taxes             --       21.7
```

```
Net income (loss)                       $209.8  $(277.0)⁴
```
(emphasis added)

Thanks to these two write-offs, Scott Paper Company reported a 1993 net loss of $277 million. If they were removed from the income statement, Scott Paper Company would have had positive net income.

OPERATIONS RESTRUCTURING

Operations restructuring expenses occur when a company tries to reorganize its operations to either increase revenue, reduce expenses, or increase productivity. They result from the following:

- Employee layoffs.
- Plant closing costs.

---

⁴ Scott Paper Company 10-K for Fiscal Year ending December 31, 1994. *http://www.sec.gov/Archives/edgar/data/87949/0000950109-95-000987.txt*. Accessed November 12, 2001.

- Production or product line modification.
- Employee training.
- Sell-off or divestiture of assets.
- Organizational changes.

During 2002 the FASB tightened the requirements for recording the costs associated with exit or disposal activities. Under FAS 146, a company can recognize a liability for a cost associated with an exit or disposal activity only "when the liability is incurred."[5] Previously, a company could record a liability as soon as it committed to a formal exit plan.

Though operations restructuring costs are normally charged as an expense against current operating income, there is an exception if the costs fall into the categories *troubled debt restructuring* or *discontinued operations,* as is explained later in this chapter.

ASSET IMPAIRMENT

Assets like buildings or machinery are considered impaired when their book value or carrying value exceeds the fair market value due to circumstances such as:

- Significant decrease in market value.
- Significant change in the way the asset is used.
- Significant cost overruns for asset construction.
- Significant adverse change in legal factors or the business climate associated with the asset.
- A projection or forecast that shows expected continuing losses associated with the asset.[6]

In addition to applying to individual assets, impairment may also apply to *asset groups.* An asset group is the lowest level for which cash flows that are largely independent of other groups can be identified. A subsidiary company that is a distinct legal entity would certainly qualify as an asset group, but an operating division or plant may also qualify.

Before impairment can be recognized, accounting standards require that the book value (balance sheet value) of a long-lived asset be more than expected future cash flows from its use and eventual disposition. For example, suppose production

---

[5] FAS 146, Accounting for Costs Associated with Exit or Disposal Activities, issued June 2002. *http://www.pwccomperio.com/search97cgi/s97is_english.dll/search97cgi/ inetsrch_english.ini?action=formgen&Template=comperio.hts.* Accessed June 2, 2003.
[6] "Accounting for the Impairment or Disposal of Long-Lived Assets." 2001. *Statement of Financial Accounting Standards No. 144.* Norwalk, CT: FASB.

machinery is carried at a current book value of $12 million but is expected to produce only operating cash flows of $1 million a year for three years and then be sold for $5 million. The asset would be considered impaired because its book value of $12 million is more than the cash flow of $8 million it is expected to generate.

If a long-lived asset meets the accounting standards impairment test, the amount by which its book value exceeds its market value may be written off as a current period loss. This loss must be reported in income from continuing operations, not as an extraordinary item.

Using the same example, if the machinery has a market value of only $4 million, the company could take a current loss of $8 million, the amount by which its book value exceeds its market value.

What if there is no independent market value for the asset because it is a unique self-constructed production machine? In that case the market value would be estimated by discounting the forecasted future cash flows at the company's current market rate of interest. If we assume a company's current market interest rate is 20 percent, then the $8 million in expected cash flows would have a present value of approximately $5 million, so the company could record a $7 million current period loss against the $12 million book value.

What this accounting option often means in practical terms is that when taking a big bath, a CEO can write off some of the cost of any long-lived assets that are not generating a cash flow that will provide a return on investment (ROI) equal to the company's current borrowing costs. This guarantees the future profitability of these assets—assuming the cash flow forecasts are reasonable.

CASE STUDY: SODAK GAMING, INC.— IMPAIRED RIVERBOAT[7]

During the fiscal year ending December 31, 1997, Sodak Gaming, Inc. wrote down the value of the "Miss Marquette" riverboat casino by approximately $9.2 million. This created a small net loss for the year after an approximately $20 million net income for the previous fiscal year. Figure 10.3 describes the company and its operations.

Figure 10.4 reproduces footnote 3 to the 1997 financial statements. It describes the impairment loss created primarily by anticipated lower profitability for the Miss Marquette.

The $9.2 million impairment loss is emphasized in Figure 10.5 (page 101), the Sodak Gaming, Inc. income statement, to make the effect clearer.

---

[7] Sodak Gaming Inc. 1997 10-K. *http://www.sec.gov/Archives/data/903856/ 0000897101-98-000348.txt.* Accessed December 6, 2001.

Figure 10.3. Sodak Gaming, Inc.: Company Operations

Sodak Gaming, Inc. (the Company or Sodak) is a leading distributor and financier of gaming equipment and a broad range
of gaming-related products and services and a provider of
wide area progressive systems, primarily to Native American
casinos. In addition, the Company operates: 1) gaming halls
and route operations in Peru beginning in May 1995; 2) a
casino entertainment facility in Quito, Ecuador, beginning
in March 1996; 3) a gaming hall in Rio de Janeiro, Brazil,
beginning in June 1996, which was converted to a route
operation in December 1997; and 4) the MISS MARQUETTE riverboat casino entertainment facility (MISS MARQUETTE) in
Marquette, Iowa, beginning in July 1996.

Figure 10.4. Sodak Gaming, Inc.: 1997 Financial Statement, Footnote 3

(3) IMPAIRMENT OF LONG-LIVED ASSETS

In the fourth quarter of 1997, in recognition of changing
economic conditions and competitive environments, the
Company re-evaluated the recoverability of certain of its
long-lived assets. In December 1997, the Company recorded a
non-cash pre-tax charge to operations resulting from **impairment of certain long-lived assets of approximately $9.2 mil-
lion.** In accordance with SFAS No. 121, the carrying values
of the impaired assets were reduced to reflect a remaining
carrying value equal to the estimated future discounted cash
flows related to the impaired assets. This impairment charge
was primarily related to MISS MARQUETTE goodwill and property and equipment. Factors leading to the impairment charge
in 1997 were that earnings and earnings before interest,
taxes, depreciation and amortization (EBITDA) at the MISS
MARQUETTE were less than those experienced prior to the
Company's acquisition, as well as the effects of increased
competition. (emphasis added)

TROUBLED DEBT RESTRUCTURING

Troubled debt is restructured when a creditor grants a concession due to a debtor's
financial difficulties. In other words, the creditor agrees to take an economic loss

Figure 10.5. Sodak Gaming Income Statements

```
SODAK GAMING, INC.
CONSOLIDATED STATEMENTS OF OPERATIONS
Years ended December 31, 1997, 1996 and 1995
```

In thousands	1997	1996	1995
REVENUE:			
Product sales	$61,683	104,512	73,173
Gaming operations	54,756	34,377	9,009
Wide area progressive systems	13,329	8,149	4,097
Financing income	7,810	7,549	6,893
Total revenue	137,578	154,587	93,172
COSTS AND EXPENSES:			
Cost of product sales	48,302	81,171	55,665
Gaming operations	54,841	29,786	2,192
Selling, general and administrative	21,716	20,445	14,531
Interest and financing costs	3,704	2,284	725
Impairment of long-lived assets (note 3)	**9,238**	0	0
Total costs and expenses	137,801	133,686	73,113
INCOME (LOSS) FROM OPERATIONS	(223)	20,901	20,059

(emphasis added)

to try to salvage something from the loan. Such concessions typically fall into one of two classes:

- Acceptance of less than the book value of the debt.
- Modification of the terms of the debt.
  - —Reduction of interest rate.
  - —Extension of debt maturity date.
  - —Reduction of face amount of the debt.
  - —Reduction or deferral of accrued interest.[8]

A troubled debt restructuring usually results in a debtor recording an accounting gain and the creditor recording a loss. The gains and losses do not have to be

---

[8] Kieso, D., J. J. Weygandt, and T. D. Warfield. 2001. *Intermediate Accounting.* New York: John Wiley & Sons, Inc., pp. 741-743.

the same because debtors use FASB Statement No. 15 for computing the gain and creditors use FASB Statement No. 114 for computing the losses. In both cases, extensive disclosures are required.

Because the gain recorded by the creditor is usually considered to be an extraordinary gain, it is separately reported as an extraordinary item at the bottom of the income statement after income from continuing operations.

Because creditor losses are usually considered operating losses, they are reported under Bad Debt Expense, an operating expense, because many creditors are financial institutions in the credit-granting business. If the creditor is a nonfinancial company that normally does not have significant bad debts, it might qualify to report the loss as an extraordinary loss.

To illustrate the usual situation, assume that Company D owes Company C $200 million on a 10-year interest-bearing note. Company D is now in financial difficulty and is having trouble paying off its debts on time. If Company C agrees to accept $150 million as an immediate cash payment to settle the $200 million debt, Company C would record a $50 million loss and Company D would record a $50 million extraordinary gain.

DISCONTINUED OPERATIONS

One disadvantage to recording asset impairment losses is that they must be reported in operating income, which is used to estimate future operating income. A loss that lowers current operating income may thus also lower the company's share price because share price is often estimated as a multiple of current operating income.

The way around this problem is to structure the asset write-off to meet the accounting criteria for discontinued operations. Although these write-offs typically result in losses, they may also result in a gain. Discontinued operations gains and losses due to disposal of assets are reported in a separate section at the bottom of the income statement after operating income. In loss situations, this means that operating income will be higher because the losses are not applied against it. The reverse will be true for gain situations.

To qualify as discontinued operations, the operations and cash flows to be disposed of must be a clearly distinguishable "component" of an entity: It must be both physically and operationally separable from other company activities. It cannot refer simply to disposal of part of a line of business, a mere shifting to another location of production or marketing activities, or the phase-out of a product line or class of service. Any of the following may qualify as a component:

- Reportable segment (defined in FASB 131).
- Operating segment (defined in FASB 131).
- Reporting unit (defined in FASB 142).
- Asset group (defined in FASB 144).

Suppose a cereal company in Chicago, Illinois, decided to sell a money-losing electronics division that operated in Los Angeles, California, as a totally separated subsidiary. The sale would qualify as a discontinued operation. The cereal company could then record a loss in the current fiscal period for estimated losses on sale of the division—even though a sale may not be expected until the next fiscal year.

Assume that in mid-December the cereal company's board of directors approved a plan to sell the electronics division. The electronics division had a recorded book value of $50 million but was expected to sell for only $20 million, so there would be a $30 million loss on the sale. The plan estimated that it would take six months to find a buyer at $20 million and that the division would have to be operated at a loss of $10 million during those six months. The cereal company could record a $30 million discontinued operation loss in its December 31st financial statements even though this loss would be incurred in the next fiscal year. It could also classify and report in the Discontinued operations segment of the income statement any losses incurred during that fiscal year from operating the electronics division. The $10 million estimated future operating loss would have to be recorded in the future Discontinued operations category as it was incurred.

Figure 10.6 shows an example from FASB 144 of how a discontinued operations loss should be reported at the bottom of the income statement.[9]

Figure 10.6. Reporting Discontinued Operations

Income from continuing operations before income taxes	$XXXX
Income taxes	XXX
Income from continuing operations	$XXXX
Discontinued operations (Note X)	
Loss from operations of discontinued Component	
X (including loss on disposal of $XXX)	XXXX
Income tax benefit	XXXX
Loss on discontinued operations	XXXX
Net income	$XXXX

CASE STUDY: SPINNAKER INDUSTRIES, INC. SALE[10]

This case study involves a gain, rather than the more common loss, on discontinued operations. On July 30, 1999 Spinnaker Industries Inc., a manufacturer of adhesive-backed paper label stock for the packaging industry, completed the sale

---

[9] "Accounting for the Impairment or Disposal of Long-Lived Assets." 2001. *Statement of Financial Accounting Standards No. 144.* Norwalk, CT: FASB, Paragraph 43.

[10] Spinnaker Industries Inc. 10-K for Fiscal Year ending December 31, 1999. *http://www. sec.gov/Archives/edgar/data/314865/0000912057-00-014916-index.html.* Accessed November 29, 2001.

of its industrial tape business to Intertape Polymer Group Inc. for $105 million in cash and warrants valued at $3 million. This produced an after-tax gain on sale of approximately $18 million.

The after-tax gain on sale would be computed as follows:

Assets

Approximate net current assets of discontinued business	$39 million	
Approximate net non-current assets of discontinued business	$72 million	
Total assets		$111 million

Liabilities

Approximate net current liabilities of discontinued business	($18) million	
Approximate net non-current liabilities of discontinued business	($6) million	
Estimated other liabilities	($3) million	
Total liabilities		($27) million

Approximate book value of discontinued business	**$84 million**
Selling price for discontinued business	$108 million
Approximate before-tax gain on sale	$24 million
Approximate tax expense on sale	($6) million
Approximate after-tax gain on sale	$18 million

In accordance with GAAP, the after-tax gain of $18 million was reported at the bottom of the income statement in Discontinued Operations, after Operating Income. This gain is the principal reason that Spinnaker reported 1999 net income of approximately $12 million instead of an operating loss of $5 million. An added benefit was that the any future operating losses from the discontinued business will not be reported in Spinnaker's income statements. The losses leading up to the sale were $1.438 million for 1999, $3.813 million for 1998, and $1.102 million for 1997. They constituted the bulk of Spinnaker's losses for those years.

Figure 10.7 shows how the sale was reported on the Spinnaker financial statements. It was accompanied by the statement shown in Figure 10.8.

In summary, Spinnaker Industries, Inc. was able to use the discontinued operations provisions of GAAP to remove its money-losing industrial tape business from its operating revenues and expenses statements and report a positive net income of $12 million instead of a $5 million loss . This put the company in a more favorable financial light.

Figure 10.7. Spinnaker Consolidated Statements of Operations

SPINNAKER INDUSTRIES, INC. AND SUBSIDIARIES

CONSOLIDATED STATEMENTS OF OPERATIONS

	YEAR ENDED DECEMBER 31,		
	1999	1998	1997
	(IN THOUSANDS, EXCEPT PER SHARE DATA)		
Net sales......................	$162,082	$159,135	$112,237
Cost of sales..................	148,703	141,430	98,596
Gross profit	13,379	17,705	13,641
Selling, general and administrative expenses.........	11,797	12,427	9,531
Income from operations...........	1,582	5,278	4,110
Interest expense	11,485	8,228	4,706
Other income (expense)-net.......	2,286	(65)	47
Loss from continuing operations before income taxes, discontinued operations and extraordinary gain.............	(7,617)	(3,015)	(549)
Income tax benefit (provision)...	2,431	209	(136)
Loss from continuing operations before discontinued operations and extraordinary gain.........	(5,186)	(2,806)	(685)
Discontinued operations:			
Loss from discontinued operations, net of income tax benefit	**(1,438)**	**(3,813)**	**(1,102)**
Gain on sale of discontinued operations, net of income tax provision..................	**18,096**	--	--
Income (loss) from discontinued operations.....................	16,658	(3,813)	(1,102)
Extraordinary gain on early extinguishment of debt, net of income tax provision	603	--	--
Net income (loss)	$12,075	$(6,619)	$(1,787)
Earnings per common share—basic and assuming dilution:			
Weighted average shares outstanding....................	7,342	7,199	6,321

Figure 10.7. Spinnaker Consolidated Statements of Operations, *Cont'd*

```
Loss from continuing operations
 before discontinued operations
 and extraordinary gain.........$ (0.71)      $ (0.39)      $ (0.11)

Income (loss) from discontinued
 operations.......................2.27        (0.53)        (0.17)
Extraordinary gain .................0.08         --            --

Net income (loss) per
 common share....................$1.64$       (0.92)       $ (0.28)
```

SPINNAKER INDUSTRIES, INC. AND SUBSIDIARIES

CONSOLIDATED BALANCE SHEETS

	DECEMBER 31,	
	1999	1998
	(IN THOUSANDS, EXCEPT SHARE DATA)	
ASSETS		
Current assets:		
Cash and cash equivalents	$11,318	--
Accounts receivable, less allowance for doubtful accounts and cash discounts of $240 in 1999 and $251 in 1998	20,036	21,439
Inventories	25,920	24,217
Prepaid expenses and other	1,113	1,014
Deferred income taxes	1,406	1,211
Net current assets of discontinued operations	--	**38,605**
Total current assets	59,793	86,486
Restricted cash	56,026	--
Property, plant and equipment:		
Land	573	573
Buildings and improvements	7,999	9,746
Machinery and equipment	44,991	42,497
Accumulated depreciation	(14,977)	(11,298)
	38,586	41,518
Goodwill, net	22,020	21,075
Other assets	8,589	7,201
Net non-current assets of discontinued operations	--	**71,651**
Total assets	$185,014	$227,931

Figure 10.7. Spinnaker Consolidated Statements of Operations, *Cont'd*

```
LIABILITIES AND SHAREHOLDERS' EQUITY
Current liabilities:
  Accounts payable . . . . . . . . . . . . $12,387    $16,782
  Accrued liabilities  . . . . . . . . . . . 7,553      3,106
  Current portion of long-term debt  . . . . . 686      1,691
  Working capital revolver  . . . . . . . 20,504       42,731
  Accrued interest . . . . . . . . . . . . . 2,399      2,575
  Net current liabilities of
    discontinued Operations . . . . . . . . .     --   18,162

Total current liabilities. . . . . . . . . 43,529     85,047


Long-term debt, less current portion. . . 115,595    126,086
Net deferred income taxes . . . . . . . . . 3,890         466
Pension liabilities . . . . . . . . . . . . 1,579       1,540
Net non-current liabilities of
  discontinued operations . . . . . . . .        --     6,446

Commitments and contingencies

Shareholders' equity:
  Class A Common Stock, no par
    or stated value, authorized
    10,000,000 shares; issued 3,661,399
    Shares in 1999 and 1998 and Common
    Stock, no par or stated value,
    authorized 15,000,000 Shares;
    issued 3,871,012 in 1999 and 1998
    at designated value . . . . . . . . . . 3,124       3,124
  Additional paid-in capital  . . . . . . . 15,867     15,867
  Retained earnings (accumulated deficit). . 1,542    (10,533)
  Less cost of common stock in treasury,
    95,332 shares each of Class A Common
    Stock and Common stock in 1999 and 1998 . (112)      (112)

Total shareholders' equity . . . . . . . . 20,421       8,346

Total liabilities and shareholders'
  equity. . . . . . . . . . . . . . . . . . $185,014  $227,931
```
(emphasis added)

Figure 10.8. Spinnaker Industries, Inc.: Footnote 3

3. DISCONTINUED OPERATIONS

On April 9, 1999, the Company entered into a definitive agreement to sell its Industrial Tape Business to Intertape for approximately $105 million and five-year warrants to purchase 300,000 shares of Intertape common stock (New York Stock Exchange Symbol "ITP") at an exercise price of $29.50 per share. The warrants were valued at approximately $3.0 million using the Black-Scholes option pricing model and are reflected in other assets of continuing operations. Accordingly, operating results of the industrial tape segment have been segregated from continuing operations and reported as a separate line item on the statement of operations.

The sale of Central Products and Spinnaker Electrical assets closed on August 10, 1999 and July 30, 1999, respectively. The Company recorded gains totaling $18.1 million, net of applicable income taxes of approximately $5.9 million. The Company offset the cash tax liability by utilizing net operating loss carry-forwards.

The Company has restated its prior financial statements to present the operating results of the industrial tape segment as a discontinued operation. The industrial tape segment net sales were $69.5 million, $121.8 million and $119.7 million for the periods ended December 31, 1999, 1998, and 1997, respectively.

11 BIG BET ON THE FUTURE

This chapter discusses and illustrates two popular big bet techniques for managing earnings.

Management can actually *buy* guaranteed future earnings increases by making a big bet on the future through an acquisition. This can typically increase earnings in one of two ways:

1. Consolidating the acquired company's earnings with corporate earnings, or
2. Writing off much of the acquisition cost under In-Process Research and Development.

BUYING AN EARNINGS BOOST VIA ACQUISITION

One way to manage earnings is to simply buy them. This is done by purchasing companies or assets that increase current-period net income because they generate more current earnings than they cost to finance.

Suppose Company X buys Company Y for a total price of $400 million. Before the acquisition Company Y had assets of $300 million and was generating $30 million a year in after-tax operating income. The $100 million extra in the purchase price is attributable to goodwill. Company X finances the acquisition by investing $100 million of its cash and borrowing the remaining $300 million at 8 percent interest. Once the acquisition is in hand, ignoring good will, Company X will report a net earnings boost of $13.2 million, computed as follows:

A. Company Y earnings	$30.0 million
B. After-tax cost of 8% interest expense on $300 million at a 30% tax rate	($16.8 million)
C. Earnings boost for Company X	$13.2 million

WHAT ABOUT THE $100 MILLION OF GOODWILL?

Under the old GAAP, goodwill had to be amortized over a period not to exceed 40 years. If it were amortized over 20 years, the annual after-tax expense would be $3.5 million, still leaving an earnings boost of approximately $10 million earnings ([$100 million/20 years = $5 million per year amortization] x 70% after-tax cost rate = $3.5 million]). Since 2002, new GAAP related to goodwill applies. FASB 142 says that goodwill does not have to be amortized at all unless it becomes impaired or otherwise loses value in some way—so for an acquisition in 2003, Company X can report the entire $13. 2 million earnings increase.

WHAT IF THE PURCHASE WERE FINANCED SOLELY WITH THE STOCK OF COMPANY X?

If Company X bought the stock of Company Y solely with its own shares, there would be no debt incurred and therefore no interest cost. Under new GAAP, the $30 million of after-tax earnings would flow straight into the net income of Company X, which would report an earnings increase for the year.

An important question here, however, is "Would the *earnings per share* (EPS) of Company X also increase?" The answer depends on how many shares of its own stock Company X had to issue to buy Company Y. Obviously, the fewer, the better the deal for Company X. The implied P/E ratio for the Company Y acquisition is 13.3 ($400 million price/$30 million earnings). As long as Company X's pre-acquisition P/E ratio is higher than 13.3 and earnings are stable, post-acquisition EPS for Company X will increase. For example, if Company X had a P/E ratio of 15 and acquired Company Y for a P/E of 13.3, the post-acquisition EPS of Company X would increase because Company X would be buying cheaper earnings as measured by the P/E ratio. This phenomenon has been summarized by John Brooks:

> *"The simple mathematical fact is that anytime a company with a high multiple buys one with a lower multiple, a kind of magic comes into play. Earnings per share of the new, merged company in the first year of its life come out higher than those of the acquiring company in the previous year, even though neither company does any more business than before. There is an apparent growth in earnings that is entirely an optical illusion."* [1]

---

[1] Brooks, John. 1973. *The Go-Go Years.* New York: John Wiley & Sons.

CASE STUDY: GENERAL ELECTRIC ACQUISITIONS

General Electric Co. has had one of the premier smooth earnings growth records. The company has been able to achieve this through fundamental growth in its business units and through careful attention to earnings growth. Some years ago the *Wall Street Journal* explained:

> *"Another way GE manages its earnings is by literally buying them—by acquiring companies or assets that are immediately profitable because they throw off more income than GE's cost of financing. Much of the growth in GE Capital's earnings in the past few years has been generated by a spate of acquisitions.*
>
> *Of course we're buying earnings when we do an acquisition," says James Parke, GE Capital's chief financial officer. The financial-services subsidiary acquired assets totaling $16.9 billion in 1993 alone.*
>
> *Daniel Porter, GE Capital's North American chief of retailer financial services, says he and his colleagues may hunt for acquisitions if his division might miss its annual earnings target. He says they ask: "Gee, doesn't somebody else have some income? Is there some other deal we can make?"*[2]

CASE STUDY: WORLDCOM INC.—ACQUISITION OF MCI

Before the recent financial debacle, WorldCom (now emerging from bankruptcy as once again MCI) was one of the largest telecommunications companies in the United States and served local, long distance and Internet customers internationally as well as domestically. Organized in 1983, the company provided telecommunications services to business, government, telecommunications companies and consumer customers through its networks of primarily fiberoptic cables, digital microwave, and fixed and transportable satellite earth stations.[3]

On September 14, 1998, the WorldCom, Inc. acquired MCI Communications Corporation for approximately $40 billion in stock. In 1997 revenues for WorldCom were $7,384 million versus $19,653 million for MCI. Assets of WorldCom at December 31, 1997, were $22,389 million versus for $25,510 mil-

---

[2] Smith, R., S. Lipin, and A. K. Naj. "Managing Profits: How General Electric Damps Fluctuations in Its Annual Earnings." *Wall Street Journal*, November 3, 1994.

[3] MCI Worldcom 10-K for Fiscal Year Ended December 31, 1998. *http://www.sec.gov/Archives/edgar/data/723527/0000950134-99-002242.txt.* Accessed November 14, 2001.

lion for MCI.[4] WorldCom's 1997 EPS were $0.40[5] while MCI's were $0.22.[6] Before the acquisition WorldCom had a P/E ratio of 115. MCI's P/E ratio was 22.[7] This large disparity in P/E ratios gave WorldCom a huge incentive to acquire MCI in order to increase EPS.

In 1999, the first full fiscal year after the acquisition, MCIWorldCom revenues were $37,120 million, net income was $3,941 million, and EPS were $1.40.[8] Figure 11.1 shows the dramatic increase in WorldCom stock during 1998.

Figure 11.1. WorldCom Stock Price Changes in 1998[9]

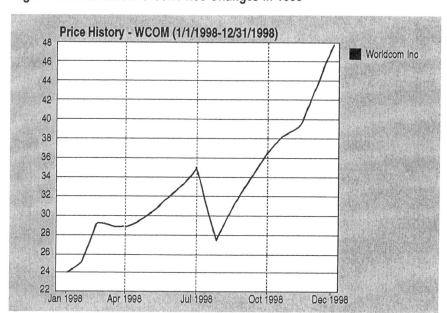

---

[4] MCI Communications Corp. 10-K for Fiscal Year Ended December 31, 1997. http://www.sec.gov/Archives/edgar/data/64079/0000064079-98-000013.txt. Accessed November 14, 2001.
[5] Worldcom Inc. 10-K for Fiscal Year Ended December 31, 1997. http://www.sec.gov/ Archives/edgar/data/723527/0000950134-98-002566.txt. Accessed November 14, 2001.
[6] Op. cit., note 5.
[7] Spiro, L. N. "Commentary: WorldCom : Paper Tiger?" *Business Week.* http://www.businessweek.com/1997/42/b3549101.htm. Accessed November 14, 2001.
[8] MCI Worldcom 10-K for Fiscal Year Ending December 31, 1999. http://www.sec.gov/Archives/edgar/data/723527/0000931763-00-000735-index.html. Accessed November 14, 2001.
[9] MSN Money. http://moneycentral.msn.com/investor/charts/chartdl.asp?Symbol= us%3aWCOM. Accessed November 14, 2001.

IN-PROCESS R&D WRITE-OFF

When a company is acquired under a business combination accounted for as a purchase transaction, the purchase price is presumed to be paid for the fair market value of identifiable assets, both tangible and intangible. These assets are then written off over time as depreciation or amortization expenses against revenues over the years that benefit from the use of the assets.

Future earnings can be relieved of this expense write-off if some of the purchase price can be written off as an expense immediately. In Process Research and Development (IPRD) provides an opportunity for this immediate write-off. Ever since FASB Statement No. 2 was issued in 1974, GAAP required companies to expense R&D costs even though the purpose of R&D expenditures is to create a economic asset.[10] The FASB believed that because valuation of R&D is extremely difficult, in the interests of objectivity, all R&D costs should simply be expensed as incurred.

A GAAP interpretation issued in 1975 states that R&D costs acquired during business combinations accounted for as a purchase transactions are to receive the same accounting treatment—immediate write-off.[11] This interpretation is the basis for the IPRD write-off.

Assume Company A acquires Company B for $100 million in cash in a straight purchase transaction. Company A would be expected to record $100 million of assets on its balance sheet because it is giving up $100 million in cash. If the only assets of Company B, the acquired company, were plant assets worth $100 million, Company A would have to record these plant assets at $100 million and depreciate them over their expected useful lives. If the average life of the assets was 10 years and straight-line depreciation were used, Company A would for the next 10 years face an annual drag on future earnings of the $10 million of annual depreciation expense.

But what if Company B had only $10 million in plant assets and $90 million of IPRD projects? The $90 million could be written off immediately as a special one-time charge against earnings. The annual future drag on Company A's earnings for the next 10 years would then be only $1 million of depreciation expense per year. Because Company A's future operating income would then be higher, presumably its share price would also be higher.

Professor Baruch Lev studied 722 companies that used R&D expensing and found that median earnings rose 1.29 percent in the fourth quarter after the deal but would have risen just 0.31 percent if the acquisition costs had been amortized over four years. Median return on equity rose 4.84 percent, well above the 3.54 ROE

---

[10] Financial Accounting Standards Board. 1974. *Statement of Financial Accounting Standards No. 2—Accounting for Research and Development Costs.*
[11] Financial Accounting Standards Board. 1975. *FASB Interpretation No. 4—Applicability of FASB Statement No. 2 to Business Combinations Accounted for by the Purchase Method.*

that would have resulted with amortization. This clearly shows that expensing IPRD can generously boost future earnings.[12]

CASE STUDY: YAHOO!—IN-PROCESS R&D WRITE-OFF

In June 1998, Yahoo acquired software maker Viaweb in a stock exchange valued at $49 million. Of this amount, Yahoo immediately took a $45 million (91 percent) deduction against earnings for in-process research and development, rather than amortizing the cost against future earnings over a number of years. This kept the cost of the acquisition from lowering net income in future years. It was estimated that "if Yahoo! had to amortize the cost of Viaweb over seven years, it would trim 10 cents a share a year from Yahoo! earnings at a time the company is just moving toward profitability."[13] The GAAP-allowed write-off of in process research and development will thus make Yahoo's future financial statement look significantly better.

CASE STUDY: IBM CORPORATION AND LOTUS DEVELOPMENT

In July 1995, International Business Machines (IBM) bought Lotus Development Corporation (Lotus) for $3.2 billion. IBM was a major computer manufacturer, in existence since 1914, with 1994 revenues of $32 billion and assets of $81 billion. Lotus was a Boston-based software company founded in 1982 with 1994 revenues of $971 million and assets of $904 million.

Lotus's first major software product had been Lotus 1-2-3, an electronic spreadsheet, introduced in November 1982. It was an immediate success. In 1983, its first full year in operation, Lotus sales were $53 million. Lotus later developed a variety of other software products, including a mail-forwarding software package and Notes, a popular groupware package that allowed multiple remote users to share data.

IBM accounted for the acquisition of Lotus under the Purchase accounting method, where the identifiable tangible (cash, receivables, inventory, land, equipment, etc.) and intangible assets (trademarks, patents, employee agreement, leaseholds, etc.) bought are recorded at fair market value on the books of the acquirer. Any purchase price in excess of these fair market values is recorded as goodwill. At the time of this acquisition goodwill was generally amortized against future earnings over a period of up to 40 years.

On IBM's 1995 financial statements, independent appraisals established the following values for the various asset classes of Lotus:

[12] Willis, G. SmartMoney.com: Market Insider, August 03, 2000.
http://www.smartmoney.com/print/in...%Findex%Ecfm%Fstory%3D199807302.
[13] Willis, G. SmartMoney.com: Market Insider, August 3, 2000.
http://www.smartmoney.com/print/in...%Findex%Ecfm%Fstory%3D199807302.

(DOLLARS IN MILLIONS)

Tangible net assets	$ 325
Identifiable intangible assets	542
Current software products	290
Purchased in-process research and development	1,840
Goodwill	540
Deferred tax liabilities related to identifiable intangible assets	(291)
Total	$3,246"[14]

In keeping with GAAP, IBM wrote off the $1,840 million of IPRD costs against third quarter 1995 earnings. Though it is hard to assess the precise boost this had on future IBM earnings, A. J. Briloff, a noted accounting professor, estimated that the after-tax effect "would be equal to about $401 million—which also would equal 10 percent of IBM's $3.84 billion bottom line for 1996's first nine months."[15] Figure 11.2 (page 116) shows the dramatic rise in IBM's stock price during the 1995-1996 period. Much of the disproportionate stock price increase was undoubtedly due to other factors, but the sudden 10 percent earnings boost surely did no harm.

Figure 11.2. IBM Stock Price Rise, 1995-1996[16]

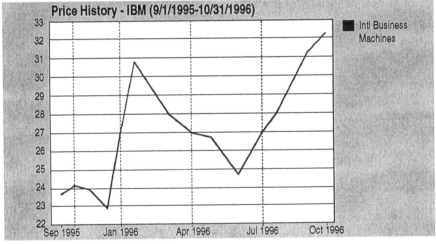

[14] International Business Machines Corp. 10-K for Fiscal Year Ending December 31, 1995. *http://www.sec.gov/Archives/edgar/data/51143/0000950112-96-000889.txt.* Accessed November 14, 2001

[15] Briloff, A. J. "Big Blue Haze—How Accounting for the Lotus Takeover Allows IBM to Inflate Profits." *Barron's,* December 23, 1996, p. 17.

[16] MSN Money. *http://moneycentral.msn.com/investor/charts/chartdl.asp?Symbol= ibm&ShowChtBt=Refresh+Chart&DateRangeForm=1&PT=8&CP=1&C5=9&C6=1995 &C7=10&C8=1996&C9=2&ComparisonsForm=1&CE=0&CompSyms=&DisplayForm =1&D9=1&D0=1&D4=1&D7=&D6=&D3=0.* November 14, 2001.

12 FLUSHING THE INVESTMENT PORTFOLIO

This chapter illustrates various popular techniques for managing earnings by flushing the investment portfolio.

One key to successfully managing earnings is to be able to easily time the application of a given technique. Flushing the investment portfolio may well be the easiest technique to time. Often all an executive has to do is pick up the telephone and instruct the corporate treasurer to sell specific securities that will help the company generate the gain or the loss it needs at the moment to manage earnings up or down. To make sure the intended result is achieved, however, the executive must understand the complicated GAAP requirements.

GAAP AND INVESTMENT SECURITIES

Under current GAAP, (a) all investments in debt securities (bonds, commercial paper, government securities, etc.) and (b) those investments in equity securities (common stock, preferred stock, etc.) that comprise less than 20 percent of the total equity security issue are classified into one of three categories—each of which evokes a different way of recognizing gains and losses, as is shown in Table 12.1.

GAAP affords management some opportunity to engage in "gains trading" (otherwise known as "cherry picking"). Those who want to manage income upward may sell their winners and hold on to their losers. They will do the opposite if they want to manage their income downward. This is particularly true for debt securities in the held-to-maturity category because they are carried at amortized cost rather than market value.[1]

Table 12.1. Recognition of Gains and Losses on Investment Securities.

Category	Unrealized Gains & Losses	Realized Gains & Losses
Trading	Recognized	Recognized
Held-to maturity	Not recognized	Recognized
Available-for-sale	Recognized only in comprehensive income, not net income	Recognized

To fully understand the significance of the reporting categories for investment securities, the manager must recognize the GAAPrequires not one but two reported incomes.

COMPREHENSIVE VERSUS NET INCOME

The all-inclusive concept of income has become the accepted way of measuring financial performance. This basically demands that all revenues, expenses, gains, and losses are recognized in income.

Due to both political pressure and disagreements over accounting theory, the rulemaking bodies that establish GAAP(currently the FASB) have established exceptions that permit certain items to bypass the income statement altogether. Somewhat unbelievably, this has resulted in two definitions of income under current GAAP:

1. *Net income* reflects all revenue and expense items reported on the income statement.

2. *Comprehensive income*[2] includes net income plus any other gains or losses that might bypass the income statement due to GAAP rules.

Net Income is displayed at the bottom of the income statement. It is the number investors traditionally look at in measuring financial performance.

Comprehensive Income may be reported in any of three ways:

1. On a second, separate income statement.

2. At the bottom of the traditional income statement after Net Income.

3. In the Statement of Stockholders' Equity.

---

[1] Kieso, D. E., J. J. Weygandt, and T. D. Warfield. 2001. *Intermediate Accounting*, 10th ed. New York: John Wiley & Sons, Inc., p. 940.

[2] FASB, "Reporting Comprehensive Income." *Statement of Financial Accounting Standards No. 130*. Norwalk, CT: FASB, June 1997.

Most companies opt to bury Comprehensive Income in the Statement of Stockholders' Equity. They believe the other two options are confusing to investors because they obscure reported Net Income, the traditional measure of financial performance.

TYPES OF INVESTMENT IN SECURITIES

GAAPrequires management to classify investment securities into one of the three following categories, each with its own rules for reporting gains or losses.

TRADING SECURITIES

Trading securities may be either debt or equity securities, as long as they comprise less than 20 percent of a total stock issue, that are primarily held for the short term, either as a place to park excess funds or to generate trading profits. The time frame for holding these securities would generally be no more than three months.

These securities are reported in the balance sheet at fair market value. Any unrealized holding gains or losses are reported in net income, even though the security has not been sold. When a trading security is sold, an additional gain or loss will be recorded for any change in value that has occurred since the date of the last balance sheet.

Since the practical effect of the GAAP rules for trading securities is that they are marked-to-market value daily, this category of investment securities offers no significant opportunity for earnings management.

HELD-TO-MATURITY SECURITIES

Held-to-maturity securities are simply long-term debt securities. This category does not apply to equity securities because by definition there is no maturity date for equity securities. This category applies only to a debt security that a company both intends and has the ability to hold for the long term. For example, if a company bought a 10-year bond planning to hold it until maturity, the bond would be classified as a held-to-maturity security—unless the company did not have the ability to keep it 10 years. Lack of ability to hold the security might apply if the company's liquidity needs were likely to force sale of the bond before maturity or if there is an interest rate or foreign exchange risk associated with the bond that the company might not be able to tolerate.

Held-to-maturity securities are carried on the balance sheet at amortized cost. This means that any premium or discount incurred on purchase of the security is amortized into the income statement over the life of the security.

For these securities, no gain or loss is recognized for year-to-year market-caused fluctuations in value. Gains or losses on these securities are recognized only when they are actually sold.

You may well be wondering how these securities can be used for earnings management purposes if they are to be held to a specific maturity date. In fact, they do offer a small opportunity due to some GAAP exceptions related to what actually constitutes "held-to-maturity." One exception arises when the security has been held long enough so that interest rate risk is no longer an important factor in its pricing, for example, three months before maturity. Another exception arises when at least 85 percent of the principal has been collected. At that point, the security is considered to have been held to maturity. These exceptions offer a little wiggle room, but not much.

AVAILABLE-FOR-SALE SECURITIES

Available-for-sale securities may be either debt or equity investments, comprising less that 20 percent of a total stock issue, that do not fall into either the trading or held-to-maturity classifications. In other words, this is the catch-all classification.

These securities are reported in the balance sheet at fair market value. Any unrealized holding gains or losses are reported in Other Comprehensive Income, *not* Net Income, even though the security has not been sold. When an available-for-sale security is actually sold, the realized cumulative gains or losses are then reported in Net Income.

CASE STUDY: PFIZER CORPORATION INVESTMENT DISCLOSURES[3]

Pfizer Inc. is a research-based, global pharmaceutical company that discovers, develops, manufactures, and markets both innovative medicines for humans and animals and many well-known consumer products. The Pfizer annual report for the fiscal year ending December 31, 2000, demonstrates how information about debt and equity security investments is presented.

Section A of Footnote 6-Financial Instruments from the Pfizer annual report is shown in Figure 12.1, which breaks out how Pfizer's $7,937 million in investments were spread between trading, held-to-maturity, and available-for-sale securities.

---

[3] Pfizer Inc. 10-K for Fiscal Year Ending December 31, 2000. *http://www.sec.gov/ Archives/edgar/data/78003/000095012301002716/y46668e10-k405.htm.* Accessed December 1, 2001.

Figure 12.1. Pfizer Investment Allocations

A. Investments in Debt and Equity Securities

Information about our investments follows:

	December 31, 2000 (millions of dollars)
Trading securities	$ 110
Amortized cost and fair value of held-to-maturity debt securities:*	
Corporate debt	5,597
Certificates of deposit	674
Total held-to-maturity debt securities	6,271
Cost and fair value of available-for-sale debt securities*	1,089
Cost of available-for-sale equity securities	151
Gross unrealized gains	326
Gross unrealized losses	(10)
Fair value of available-for-sale equity securities	467
Total investments	$7,937

Gross unrealized gains and losses are not significant.

These investments are in the following captions in the balance sheet:

	December 31, 2000 (millions of dollars)
Cash and cash equivalents	$ 658
Short-term investments	5,764
Long-term loans and investments	1,515
Total investments	$7,937

Notice how the footnote shown in the figure first described components of the three investment security captions—trading, held-to-maturity, and available-for-sale—totaling $7,937 million. Since these investments are not reported in the balance sheet with the same captions, it then showed us which captions in the balance sheet did reflect the $7,937 million.

In Figure 12.2, the Pfizer balance sheet, you can trace $5,764 million of the value in Short-term Investments, but neither the Cash and Cash Equivalents amount of $658 million or the Long-term Loans and Investments amount of $1,515 million can be seen because for balance sheet presentation, they were combined with other accounts.

Figure 12.2. Consolidated Balance Sheet

```
Pfizer Inc. and Subsidiary Companies
```
                                                December 31, 2000
                                  (millions, except per share data)

```
Assets
  Current Assets
  Cash and cash equivalents                    $    1,099
  Short-term investments                            5,764
  Accounts receivable, less allowance
    for doubtful accounts:
    2000—$274; 1999—$230                            5,489
  Short-term loans                                    140
  Inventories
    Finished goods                                  1,195
    Work in process                                 1,074
    Raw materials and supplies                        433

    Total inventories                              2,702

  Prepaid expenses and taxes                        1,993

    Total current assets                          17,187
  Long-term loans and investments                  2,529
  Property, plant and equipment, less
    accumulated depreciation                       9,425
  Goodwill, less accumulated
    amortization:2000—$300; 1999—$256             1,791
  Other assets, deferred taxes and
    deferred charges                               2,578

    Total assets                               $ 33,510
```
(emphasis added)

Pfizer's financials illustrate how hard it would be for the average investor to determine where in the balance sheet investment gains or losses can be found. It is just as hard to trace transfers between categories that would result in gains or losses being reported.

RECLASSIFYING SECURITIES IN THE INVESTMENT PORTFOLIO

Company managers can decide to move a security to a different security class. If they do so, they must accept the accounting rules for the new classification. GAAP[4] requires that transfers between any of the categories be accounted for at fair value. This can result in the kinds of impacts shown in Figure 12.3.

---

[4] FASB, "Accounting For Certain Investments in Debt and Equity Securities." *Statement of Financial Accounting Standards No. 115.* Norwalk, CT: FASB, May, 1993.

Figure 12.3. Effects of Changing Classification of a Security

Transfer Categories	Impact on Stockholders' Equity	Impact on Net Income
Trading to available-for-sale	Retained earnings increase or decrease	Any unrealized gain or loss is reported in net income.
Available-for-sale to trading	Retained earnings increase or decrease	Any unrealized gain or loss is reported in net income.
Held-to-maturity to available-for-sale	Unrealized gain or loss recognized as separate component in stockholders'equity	None.
Available-for-sale to held-to-maturity	Unrealized gain or loss carried as a separate component of stockholders'equity and amortized over the remaining life of the security	None.

Source: Kieso, D. E., J. J. Weygandt, and T. D. Warfield. 2001. *Intermediate Accounting,* 10th ed. New York:John Wiley & Sons, Inc., p. 941.

One reason a manager might change a security classification is in response to an unexpected change in the economic circumstances of the company. Suppose a company had $10 million of long-term bonds that it had intended, and had thought it had the ability, to hold to maturity. Three years after the bonds are bought, a severe economic downturn decreases the company's operating cash flow so much that management has to include selling the bonds in its cash operating budget for the coming year. This would cause the bonds to be reclassified from held-to-maturity to trading securities. If the bonds had appreciated in value to $14 million due to lower interest rates, the company would record a $4 million gain in net income.

Another reason a manager might change a security classification is simply a change in management intent with respect to the security. That would have the effect of moving any unrealized gain or loss on the security to or from the income statement, depending on the security's classification. Suppose the company had bought for $100 million a 10 percent stock interest in a company for speculative reasons, putting the security in the available-for-sale category. The security increased in value to $300 million. Under the available-for-sale GAAP rules, the unrealized $200 million gain in value would be reported in Other Comprehensive Income, not in Net Income. Management might decide the value increase for the security was near its peak so it would dispose of this investment in the near future. The stock would be reclassified as a trading security, the GAAP rules for trading securities would apply, and the $200 million gain would be reported in Net Income even though the security had not actually been sold.

SECURITY IMPAIRMENT

GAAP permits a deviation from normal reporting rules for securities when they are "impaired"—i.e., when "a decline in fair value below the amortized cost basis is other than temporary."[5] An impaired security may be written down and a loss recognized in current period income.

A debt security is impaired when "it is probable that the investor will be unable to collect all amounts due according to the contractual terms."[6] An equity security is impaired when the realizable (market) value is less than the book value. Since trading securities are carried on the books at market value in any case, the impairment provisions basically apply only to investments that are held-to-maturity and available-for-sale.

Assume Company A bought $10 million of long-term bonds and classified them as available-for-sale. The bonds now have a $7 million fair market value and Company A has previously reported the $3 million loss in Comprehensive Income. Company A now determines that due to a financial crisis of the bond issuer, it is probable that Company A will not be able to collect more than $6 million on the bonds. Company A can now record a $4 million loss in current income. This loss would consist of the $3 million loss previously reported in Comprehensive Income but not on the income statement plus the additional $1 million decline in value.

CASE STUDY: MICROSOFT IMPAIRED INVESTMENT WRITE-OFF[7]

The purpose of this case is to illustrate the large GAAP write-offs permitted due to security "impairment." Microsoft Corporation recorded a loss in its June 30, 2001 Income Statement for $4,800 million due to "impaired" investments.

Since it is primarily concerned with developing a wide range of software, hardware, consulting services, and other services, Microsoft has a great number of investments in the information technology sector. The general stock market decline of 2000-2001 hit this sector particularly hard.

For the 2001 fiscal year ending June 30, 2001, Microsoft's income statement reported an investment loss of $36 million (see Figure 12.4).

---

[5] FASB, "Accounting for Certain Investments in Debt and Equity Securities." *Statement of Financial Accounting Standards No. 115*. Norwalk, CT: FASB, May, 1993, Paragraph 16.
[6] FASB, "Accounting for Certain Investments in Debt and Equity Securities." *Statement of Financial Accounting Standards No. 115*. Norwalk, CT: FASB, May, 1993, Paragraph 16.
[7] Microsoft Corporation 10-K for Fiscal Year Ending June 30, 2001. *http://www.sec.gov/Archives/edgar/data/789019/000103221001501099/d10k.txt*. Accessed December 3, 2001.

Figure 12.4. Microsoft 2001 Income Statement

```
                Income Statement (In millions)
Year Ended June 30                                    2001

Revenue                                             $25,296
Operating expenses:
  Cost of revenue                                     3,455
  Research and development                            4,379
  Sales and marketing                                 4,885
  General and administrative                            857
   Total operating expenses                          13,576
Operating income                                     11,720
Losses on equity investees and other                   (159)
Investment income/(loss)                               (36)
Income before income taxes                           11,525
Provision for income taxes                            3,804
Income before accounting change                       7,721
Cumulative effect of accounting
  change (net of income taxes of $185)                 (375)
Net income                                          $ 7,346
```
(emphasis added)

The 2001 investment loss of $36 million was quite a reversal in fortunes for the company, considering that in 2000 it reported $3,326 million of investment income. The three components of the 2001 loss are shown in Figure 12.5.

Figure 12.5. Components of Microsoft 2001 Investment Loss

```
                Investment Income/(Loss)
The components of investment income/(loss) are as fol-
lows:

In Millions/Year Ended June 30                        2001
  Dividends                                         $   377
  Interest                                            1,808
  Net recognized gains/(losses) on
  investments                                        (2,221)
Investment income/(loss)                            $  (36)
```
(emphasis added)

An analysis of the footnote describing the Net Recognized Losses of $2,221 million indicates it was comprised of the following elements:

Item	Amount
Losses on Impaired Investments	*<$4,800 million>*
Losses on Derivatives	<$ 592 million>
Net Investment Gains from Sales of Titus Communications, Transpoint, and other unspecified investments	$3,171 million
Net Recognized Investment Loss	<$2,221 million>

(emphasis added)

The footnotes to the income statement provided this description of how the $4,800 million loss on impaired securities was calculated:

> *"Investments are considered to be impaired when a decline in fair value is judged to be other-than-temporary. The Company employs a systematic methodology that considers available evidence in evaluating potential impairment of its investments. In the event that the cost of an investment exceeds its fair value, the Company evaluates, among other factors, the duration and extent to which the fair value is less than cost; the financial health of and business outlook for the investee, including industry and sector performance, changes in technology, and operational and financing cash flow factors; and the Company's intent and ability to hold the investment. Once a decline in fair value is determined to be other-than-temporary, an impairment charge is recorded and a new cost basis in the investment is established. **In 2001, the Company recognized $4.80 billion in impairments of certain investments,** primarily in the cable and telecommunication industries."* (emphasis added)

In summary, GAAP permitted Microsoft to take a $4.8 billion reduction in earnings due to security impairment, even though the company continued to hold the securities that generated the impairment loss.

13 THROW OUT A PROBLEM CHILD!

This chapter illustrates techniques for managing earnings by getting rid of poorly performing subsidiaries.

One way to boost earnings boost is for a parent corporation (owner of the subsidiary) to "throw out the problem child," slang for getting rid of a poorly performing subsidiary. Doing this eliminates an earnings drag on the income statement while allowing management of the parent to concentrate attention on core competencies and operations. Disposing of a subsidiary is particularly valuable when the earnings drag seems likely to increase over time.

You can throw out a problem child using one of the following methods:

- *Sell the subsidiary.* When a subsidiary is sold, the gain or loss is reported in the current income statement. If reporting a large loss or gain is undesirable, a spin-off should be considered.

- *Create a special purpose entity (SPE).* One highly technical alternative available under GAAP is to create a qualifying special-purpose entity (SPE) and transfer financial assets to it. The assets are then deemed to have been sold and the transferor records a gain or loss on the sale. Enron Corporation allegedly inappropriately used SPEs to avoid reporting trading losses.

- *Spin off the subsidiary.* A subsidiary is spun off when its shares are distributed to or exchanged with current shareholders of the parent corporation. Thus making the shareholders, not the parent company itself, owners of the problem child. No investment-related gain or loss is normally reported on a spin-off. The parent company must, however, include the relevant gains or losses of the subsidiary as Discontinued Operations at the bottom of its current income statement. The possible operating-related negative effects of the subsidiary are then removed from all future financial statements.

To fully understand the accounting consequences of either selling or spinning off a subsidiary it is necessary first to understand the somewhat complicated GAAP reporting requirements for subsidiaries.

GAAP AND SUBSIDIARIES

Equity securities convey an ownership interest via common, preferred, or other capital stock. Table 13.1 shows the GAAP reporting requirements for the different possible levels of ownership interest that a company may have in another company.

Table 13.1. GAAP Reporting Requirements by Percentage of Ownership

Ownership %	Level of Influence	GAAP Reporting Requirement
Less than 20%	Little or none	Fair value method
20% to 50%	Significant	Equity method
More than 50%	Control	Consolidation

LESS THAN 20 PERCENT OWNERSHIP

Security ownership of less than 20 percent of total shares outstanding means that a security would fall into the GAAP requirements for investment securities that were discussed in the previous chapter. This means the security would have to be classified as either available-for-sale or trading and conform to the GAAP requirements for those categories.

TWENTY TO 50 PERCENT OWNERSHIP

When a company (or an individual) holds between 20 and 50 percent of a corporation's shares, it is presumed to have the ability to exercise significant influence over the company. GAAP requires that such securities be accounted for via the equity method, which means that the parent company must include its share of the subsidiary's net income or loss in its own income statement. This method is sometimes called "one-line consolidation" because the parent company's net income and its stockholders' equity are the same as if the subsidiary were consolidated with the parent.

Assume that P Company owns 30 percent of the common shares in S Company. For the year 2002, S Company reported $10 million net income. P Company would have had to report $3 million, its proportionate share of the $10 million, as income in its income statement for 2002, under a heading such as Income from S Company.

What happens under the equity method when S Company pays P Company a $3 million cash dividend in 2003 as a distribution of its share of the 2002 net income? Since the income had already been reported by P Company as earned in 2002, nothing would normally appear in the 2003 P Company income statement.

MORE THAN 50 PERCENT OWNERSHIP

Owning more than 50 percent of the total shares of a company is normally considered a controlling interest. This simply means that the parent company can dictate who is elected to the board of directors and hired as officers, and thereby control the operating decisions of the company.

GAAP requires that controlling interests be accounted for by consolidation. Consolidated financial statements are prepared when two or more legally separate but related companies form a single economic entity because one company controls the other. The consolidation process consists of simply adding together the financial statements of the component companies so that their activities appear to be those of a single company, even though they are legally distinct. The purpose is to present the economic substance rather than the legal form.

Consolidation generally means that all components of the subsidiary's income statement, not just its share of net income, be reported in the parent company income statement. Assume that X Company owns 100 percent of the common shares of Y Company. For 2002, Y Company reported sales revenue of $100 million, expenses of $90 million, and net income of $10 million. For consolidation, X Company would have had to add the $100 million of sales revenue to its 2002 sales revenue and report the combined total. It would also have had to add the $90 million of expenses to its 2002 expenses and report the combined total. This would have the effect of including the $10 million of Y Company net income in X Company 2002 net income.

This illustration ignores any intercompany transactions with respect to revenues or expenses. The balance sheet, statement of changes in owners' equity, and cash flow statement would also have to be consolidated.

GAAP REPORTING FOR ENTITY CHANGES

GAAPrequirements for changes in an accounting entity were specified in 1971 via APB 20.[1] The basic rule is that when there is a change in an accounting entity, the financial statements should be restated for all prior periods reported to reflect the new entity. Thus, if a new company is added to the consolidated group, the consolidated financial statements for all years reported will normally be changed to include the new company.

---

[1] Accounting Principles Board, "APB 20: Accounting Changes," July 1971, in FASB Original Pronouncements. *http://www.pwccomperio.com/search97cgi/s97is_english.dll/search97cgi/ inetsrch_english.ini?action=formgen&Template=comperio.hts.* Accessed November 29, 2001.

For example, if during 2005 Company A buys 100 percent of the stock of Company B, Company A must retroactively consolidate Company B with Company A for both 2004 and 2005 if two- year comparative financial statements are reported to shareholders.

In a year when a subsidiary is disposed of, whether by sale or spin off, the subsidiary is omitted from the balance sheet of the consolidated group because it was not a member of the consolidated group at fiscal year-end. Operating revenues and expenses of the subsidiary are removed from the operating income of the consolidated group and reported at the bottom of the income statement under Discontinued Operations. This frees Operating Income from the earnings drag created by a subsidiary that has been operating in a net loss position.

SALE OF A SUBSIDIARY

When it sells a subsidiary corporation, the parent company must record a gain or loss for the difference between the recorded book value and the selling price. The book value may be determined under either the fair value or the equity method, depending on how much of the subsidiary stock the parent owned.

The gain or loss on sale of a significant subsidiary is typically reported in Discontinued Operations, along with any operating gains or losses associated with the subsidiary. This means that these gains or losses are not included in Operating Income. Gains or losses reported in Discontinued Operations have two components:

• Gain or loss from operating the subsidiary up to the date of sale.
• Gain or loss from the sale itself.

In situations where the sale of a subsidiary is not considered significant (material) to the overall financial results, the parent company may decide not to separately disclose gains or losses on the sale. It may instead simply include such gains and losses in regular operating income. For example, in 1998 when Raytheon Co. sold its Raytheon Aircraft Montek subsidiary for $160 million in cash, it did not break out the results separately in its consolidated income statement. In fact, about the only mention of the transaction was the following footnote comment:

> *"Also in 1998, the Company sold its commercial laundry business unit for $315 million in cash and $19 million in securities, its Raytheon Aircraft Montek subsidiary for $160 million, and other non-core business operations for $273 million."*[2]

The $160 million in proceeds were less than 1 percent of Raytheon's total 1998 revenues of $19,530 million. The company presumably did not consider this amount to be material enough for separate reporting.

---

[2] Raytheon Company 10-K for Fiscal Year ended December 31, 1998. *http://www.sec.gov/ Archives/edgar/data/1047122/0001047122-99-000002.txt*. Accessed November 29, 2001.

CASE STUDY: RENAISSANCE WORLDWIDE SALE OF SUBSIDIARIES[3]

The overview to the fiscal year 2000 SEC Form 10-K for Renaissance Worldwide, Inc. reads as follows:

> "*Renaissance Worldwide, Inc. is a provider of business and information technology ("IT") consulting services. Entering 2000, the Company had four primary business units;*
>
> *(1) Information Technology Consulting Services Group,*
> *(2) the Government Solutions Group,*
> *(3) the Enterprise Solutions Group, and*
> *(4) the Business Strategy Group.*
>
> *The Company sold the Business Strategy Group on March 10, 2000 for $67.9 million and the Enterprise Solutions Group on October 20, 2000 for $78.4 million. As such, the results of operations for both of these groups have been reported as discontinued operations for all periods presented. A portion of the proceeds from these sales was used to eliminate the Company's debt under its revolving credit facility. Today, Renaissance has two stand alone operating companies: Renaissance Worldwide IT Consulting Services, Inc. ("ITCS") and GovConnect, Inc. ("GovConnect"), formerly known as the Government Solutions Group."* [4]

The gains on sale of these two subsidiaries as detailed in Footnote 4 to the financial statements are summarized in Table 13.2.

Table 13.2. Gains on Sale of Renaissance Subsidiaries

Company	Gain Net of Taxes
Business Strategy Group	$12.4 million
Enterprise Solutions Group	$23.0 million
Total gains on sales	$35.4 million

---

[3] Renaissance Worldwide Inc. 10-K for Fiscal Year Ended December 30, 2000. *http://www.sec.gov/Archives/edgar/data/1012123/000092701601001372/0000927016-01-001372-0001.txt.* Accessed November 30, 2001.

[4] Ibid.

In accordance with GAAP, a $35.465 million gain on disposal net of tax from the sale of these subsidiaries was presented after Operating Income in the Discontinued Operations section of the Renaissance Worldwide, Inc. income statement of December 30, 2000. Losses of $2.799 million from operating these subsidiaries through the date of sale were also presented in this section. Footnote 4 in its entirety read:

> Footnote 4 Describing Sale of Subsidiaries
> "4. PURCHASES AND DISPOSITIONS
>
> Fiscal 2000 Dispositions
>
> On March 10, 2000, the Company sold its **Business Strategy Group,** a management consulting practice, for $67.9 million in cash on March 10, 2000 which resulted in a gain for the Company of $12.4 million, net of $10.0 of taxes. Accordingly, the results of operations of the Business Strategy Group have been classified as discontinued operations in the accompanying financial statements (see Note 17).
>
> On October 20, 2000, the Company sold its **Enterprise Solutions Group,** a worldwide information management consulting group and provider of enterprise business solutions, for $78.4 million in cash. This transaction resulted **in a gain of $23.0 million,** net of $12.7 million of taxes. Accordingly, the results of operations of the Enterprise Solutions Group have been classified as discontinued operations in the accompanying financial statements (see Note 17)." (emphasis added)

The reporting of the sales in the income statement is shown in Figure 13.1.

QUALIFYING SPECIAL PURPOSE ENTITIES (SPEs)

GAAP permits a corporation to transfer financial assets to a qualifying SPE (new accounting standards now call these entities "variable interest entities" or VIE's) and to then record the gain or loss on the transfer and remove the assets from its balance sheet. The SPE is considered legally distinct from the transferring corporation and not under its control, thus, a sale is held to have occurred when assets are transferred. For that reason, qualifying SPEs cannot be consolidated into the financial statements of the corporation transferring the assets, while any interest retained in the transferred assets *would* have to be shown on the balance sheet. There are some restrictions, as noted in the following quote from FASB 140:

> "A qualifying SPE is demonstrably distinct from the transferor only if it cannot be unilaterally dissolved by any transferor, its affiliates, or its agents and either (a) at least 10 percent of the fair value of its beneficial interests is held by parties other than any transferor, its affiliates, or its agents or (b) the transfer is a guaranteed mortgage securitization."[5]

Figure 13.1. Excerpt from Renaissance 2000 Income Statement

Income Statement Presenting Sale of Subsidiaries

RENAISSANCE WORLDWIDE, INC
CONSOLIDATED STATEMENT OF OPERATIONS
(In thousands except per share data)

	Year Ended December 30, 2000
Revenue	$437,238
Cost of revenue	331,751
Gross profit	105,487
Selling, general and administrative expenses	135,806
Acquisition-related expenses	—
Restructuring charges and asset writedowns	18,035
Income (loss) from operations	(48,354)
Interest expense	6,113
Interest and other (income) expense, net	(1,260)
Income (loss) before taxes	(53,207)
Income tax provision (benefit)	(19,214)
Loss from continuing operations	(33,993)
Income (loss) from discontinued operations, net of income taxes	(2,799)
Gain on disposal of discontinued operations, net of tax	**35,465**
Net loss	$(1,327)

(emphasis added)

The transferring corporation can effectively control the management and distribution of the financial assets by the conditions it sets forth in the documents creating the SPE.

Moving assets to an SPE offers two opportunities for earnings management:

1. Recording the gain or loss on disposition of the assets.
2. Preventing the assets from affecting future earnings by removing them

---

[5] FASB Statement 140, *Accounting for Transfers and Servicing of Financial Assets and Extinguishments of Liabilities—A Replacement of FASB Statement No. 125,* Appendix E. http://www.pwccomperio.com/search97cgi/s97is_english.dll/search97cgi/inetsrch_ english.ini?action=formgen&Template=comperio.hts. Accessed November 24, 2001.

from the transferring corporation's balance sheet.

Financial assets that may be transferred include:

- Ownership interests.
- Contracts conveying the right to receive cash or financial instruments or exchange financial instruments on potentially favorable terms. These would include items like:
  —Securitized items, such as mortgage loans, credit card receivables, or automobile loans.
  —Receivables.

An SPE can be a trust, partnership, or other legal vehicle as long as it meets very technical GAAP conditions, including the facts that it must:

- Be distinct from the transferor.
- Be able to perform a narrow range of legal activities that are clearly speci- fied in its creation document. These activities can be changed only by approval of a majority of beneficial interest holders *other than the transferor.*
- Limit itself to holding:
  —Passive financial assets.
  —Passive derivative financial instruments.
  —Servicing rights to financial assets.
  —Temporary nonfinancial assets.
  —Cash pending distribution that has been collected from assets.[6]

SPEs AND SARBANES-OXLEY

Section 401 of the Sarbanes-Oxley Act provides that financial reports filed with the SEC "shall disclose all material off-balance sheet transactions, arrangements, obli- gations (including contingent obligations), and other relationships of the issuer with unconsolidated entities or other persons, that may have a material current or future effect on" the financial statements.[7]

This increased disclosure requirement means that companies must provide more comprehensive disclosure about unconsolidated SPEs.

CASE STUDY: LUCENT TECHNOLOGIES SPE

Lucent Technologies, Inc. was formed from the systems and technology units that were formerly a part of AT&T Corp. In April 1996, Lucent completed the initial pub- lic offering ("IPO") of its common stock and on September 30, 1996, became inde- pendent of AT&T when AT&T distributed to its shareowners all of its Lucent shares.[8]

---

[6] Ibid.

[7] HR3763, Sarbanes-Oxley Act of 2002, Section 401. *www.findlaw.com.*

[8] Lucent Technologies, Inc. 10-K for Fiscal Year Ended September 30, 2000. *http://www.sec.gov/ Archives/edgar/data/1006240/000095012300011855/y43690e10-k405.txt.* Accessed December 26, 2001.

During its fiscal year ending September 30, 2000, Lucent created a trust-based SPE to which it transferred $579 million of loans and receivables. The SPE was not consolidated in the Lucent financial statements and gains or losses on the sale were reported in operating income. This transaction is described in more detail in footnote 16 of the 2000 Lucent financial statements:

> "In September 2000, Lucent and a third-party financial institution arranged for the creation of a **non-consolidated Special Purpose Trust** (the "Trust") for the purpose of allowing Lucent from time to time to sell on a limited-recourse basis up to a maximum of $970 (million) of customer finance loans and receivables (the "Loans") at any given point in time through a wholly owned bankruptcy-remote subsidiary, which in turn will sell the Loans to the Trust. Lucent has also agreed, in the case of foreign currency denominated Loans and Loans with a fixed interest rate, to indemnify the Trust for foreign exchange losses and losses due to movements in interest rates (if any) if hedging instruments have not been entered into for such Loans. Lucent will receive a fee from the Trust for either arranging hedging instruments or providing the indemnity. Lucent will continue to service, administer and collect the Loans on behalf of the Trust and receive a fee for performance of these services. Lucent will also receive a fee for referring Loans to the Trust that the Trust purchases from Lucent. At **September 30, 2000, Lucent had sold $579 (million) of Loans to the Trust. The impact of this transaction increased cash flows from operating activities by $575 (million)."** [9] (emphasis added)

Thus, by creating an SPE and selling assets to it as permitted by GAAP, Lucent boosted its 2000 revenues by $579 million.

SPINNING OFF SUBSIDIARIES

A simple spin-off occurs when a parent company distributes shares of a subsidiary to its stockholders as a stock dividend. This means the shareholders simply receive

---

[9] Lucent Technologies, Inc. Annual Report, Fiscal Year Ended September 30, 2000. *http://www.lucent.com/investor/annual/00/notes/16.html.* Accessed December 26, 2001.

pieces of paper giving them ownership of the subsidiary and the parent receives no cash from the shareholders. A spin-off eliminates the subsidiary from the future consolidated income statement of the parent. Subsidiary operating losses for the period in which it is spun off are normally shown in Discontinued Operations at the bottom of the balance sheet, not in Operating Income.

A spun-off subsidiary is eliminated from the parent company consolidated balance sheet immediately after the effective date of the spin-off, after which time it is no longer part of the consolidated company. A spin-off can also be used to get rid of corporate assets without having to record a gain or loss on the assets, even when no subsidiary originally existed: Corporate management can create a subsidiary, put the assets in it, and then spin it off. Consider the following:

> *"Big Company owns and operates a mall and a retail store that occupies the anchor store position in that mall. The mall and the store are managed by two separate divisions. The shareholders of Big Company would like to split Big Company into two companies so that each can focus on its own operations. To achieve this, Big Company transfers the mall's assets and operations into a newly created subsidiary, Mall Company, and distributes the shares of Mall Company to its shareholders on a pro rata basis in a spinoff."*[10]

Spin-offs can be tax free under Section 355 of the Internal Revenue Code if the following conditions are met:

- More than 80 percent of the stock of the subsidiary stock is distributed to shareholders.
- The parent and subsidiary continue to engage in the same business.
- The parent has held the subsidiary stock for at least five years if it was originally purchased.
- There is a sound business reason behind the spin-off other than profit distribution.

Companies normally seek an advance ruling from the IRS on tax-free status before completing a spin-off. Spinning off a subsidiary to existing shareholders rather than selling it in an IPO avoids the sometimes onerous IPO process and the associated expenses. However, an SEC filing is still required.

Spin-offs are particularly valuable to shareholders when the stock market has undervalued the subsidiary because the unrecognized value then accrues to them. This might not happen if there was an IPO.[11]

---

[10] EITF 02-11. *Accounting For Reverse Spinoffs,* Paragraph 1. *http://www.pwccomperio. com/search97cgi/s97is_english.dll/search97cgi/inetsrch_english.ini?action=formgen&Tem plate=comperio.hts.* Accessed December 26, 2001.
[11] Frank, K. E. "Making Sense of Spin-Offs, Tracking Stock, and Equity Carve-Outs." *Strategic Finance,* Vol. 83, No. 6, December 2001, pages 38-43.

CASE STUDY: 3M SPIN-OFF OF IMATION CORP.

In 1996 Minnesota Mining and Manufacturing Company (3M) spun off its Imation Corp. data storage and imaging business to 3M's shareholders. The spin-off qualified as a tax-free stock distribution; 3M shareholders received one share of Imation Corp. common stock for every 10 shares of 3M Company stock they owned.

The principal effects of the Imation Corp. spin-off were that:

- Net losses of Imation Corp. totaling $205 million for 1994, 1995, and 1996 were shown on the 3M Company income statement as Discontinued Operations, not in Operating Income.
- 3M net income after 1996 was not affected by Imation income or losses.
- 3M stockholders'equity was reduced by $1,008 million due to the stock dividend.
- The 3M December 31, 1996, balance sheet did not reflect assets or liabilities of the subsidiary because the spin-off took place before the end of the fiscal year.

The apparent effects of the spin-off on stock price are suggested in Figure 13.2.

Figure 13.2. 3M Stock Price versus S&P 500 Index, January 1995-April 1997[12]

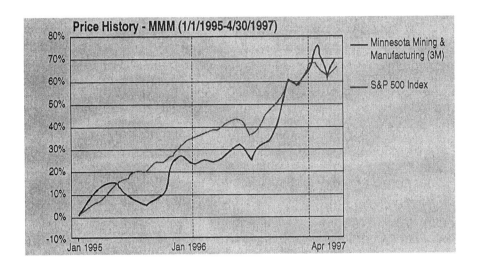

[12] MSN Money. *http://moneycentral.msn.com/investor/charts/chartdl.asp?Symbol= mmm&ShowChtBt=Refresh+Chart&DateRangeForm=1&PT=8&CP=1&C5=1&C6=199 5&C7=4&C8=1997&C9=2&ComparisonsForm=1&CB=1&CE=0&CompSyms=&Displa yForm=1&D9=1&D0=1&D4=1&D7=&D6=&D3=0.* Accessed November 29, 2001.

The 1996 3M annual report contained a footnote describing the spin-off of Imation Corp.[13] (The effect on the 3M income statements is shown in Figures 13.3.)

"*Discontinued Operations*

In November 1995, the Board of Directors approved a plan to launch the company's data storage and imaging businesses as an independent, publicly owned company and to discontinue 3M's audio and video business. In June 1996, the Board of Directors approved the tax-free distribution by 3M of the common stock of Imation Corp. (Imation) as a special dividend of one share of Imation common stock for every 10 shares of outstanding 3M common stock held of record as of the close of business on June 28, 1996. The company recorded the special dividend of Imation common stock by reducing retained earnings by $1.008 billion, which represented the carrying value of the net assets underlying the common stock distributed. The company's consolidated financial statements and notes report Imation and the audio and video business as discontinued operations.

Income from operations of the discontinued businesses for 1995 include results through November 30, 1995. Income from operations of discontinued businesses included interest expense allocations (based on the ratio of net assets of discontinued operations to consolidated net assets plus debt) of $15 million and $17 million in 1995 and 1994, respectively.

The 1995 loss on disposal of $373 million included the estimated future results of operations through the estimated date of the spin-off or closure. Major components of the loss on disposal include $300 million of severance costs and $265 million of asset write-downs, net of deferred income taxes of $232 million. The loss on disposal calculation included $13 million of interest expense. Net cash provided by discontinued operations in 1995 differs from the loss from discontinued operations principally due to two factors—the loss on disposal for which no cash had been expended at December 31, 1995, and depreciation. The $10 million 1996 gain on disposal reflects final adjustments to the company's 1995 estimated loss on disposal."

---

[13] Minnesota Mining and Manufacturing 10-K for fiscal year ending December 31, 1996. *http://www.sec.gov/Archives/edgar/data/66740/0000066740-97-000003.txt.* Accessed November 29, 2001.

Figure 13.3. Effect of Imation Sale on 3M Income Statements

Consolidated Statement of Income

Minnesota Mining and Manufacturing Company and Subsidiaries

Years ended December 31	1996	1995	1994
(Amounts in millions, except per-share amounts)			
Net sales	$14,236	$13,460	$12,148

(Other income statement details omitted for reasons of brevity)

	1996	1995	1994
Income from continuing operations	1,516	1,306	1,207
Discontinued operations			
Income from operations of discontinued businesses, net of income taxes	—	43	115
Gain (loss) on disposal of discontinued businesses, net of income taxes	10	(373)	—
Net income	$1,526	$976	$1,322

Imation Corp. Effect on 3M Income Statement

Discontinued Operations

(Millions)	1996	1995	1994
Net sales	$—	$2,645	$2,931
Income before income taxes and minority interest	—	59	143
Provision for income taxes	—	23	40
Minority interest	—	(7)	(12)
Income from operations, net of income taxes	—	43	115
Gain (loss) on disposal, net of income taxes	10	(373)	—
Total discontinued operations, net of income taxes	**$10**	**$(330)**	**$115**

Figure 13.3. Effect of Imation Sale on 3M Income Statements, *Cont'd*

Imation Corp. Assets Which Were Included In 3M Balance Sheet

Net Assets of Discontinued Operations

(Millions)	1996	1995
Current assets	$—	$1,212
Property, plant and equipment - net	—	456
Other assets	—	192
Current liabilities	—	(357)
Other liabilities	—	(95)
Net assets of discontinued operations	**$—**	**$1,408**

Decrease in 3M Stockholders' Equity Due To 1996 Imation Corp. Spinoff [14]

Consolidated Statement of Changes in Stockholders' Equity

Minnesota Mining and Manufacturing Company and Subsidiaries

Year ended December 31, 1996
(Dollars in millions, except per-share amounts)

Retained earnings	
Balance at beginning of year	$9,164
Net income	1,526
Dividends paid (per share: $1.92, $1.88, $1.76)	(803)
Special dividend of Imation Corp. common stock	**(1,008)**
Effects of stock option and benefit plans	(123)
Balance at end of year	$8,756

(emphasis added)

---

[14] Ibid.

14 IF YOU DON'T LIKE A GAAP, CHANGE IT!

For many areas of financial statements, there is more than one possible method of accounting. This chapter explains how management may elect to apply different GAAP.

Some executives believe that once a company is using a particular accounting method, it is stuck with it permanently. This is not true. GAAP actually permits companies to change accounting methods whenever they believe that the new method *better reflects economic reality.*

A change in accounting methods may be any of the following:

- Change in accounting principle.
- Change in accounting estimate.
- Change in reporting entity.

CHANGE IN ACCOUNTING PRINCIPLE

There is a basic presumption in GAAP that once an accounting principle has been adopted it "should not be changed in accounting for events and transactions of a similar type."[1] The idea is to enhance comparability and facilitate year-to-year analysis through consistent application of GAAP.

A business may, however, change accounting principles if it can build a case that the new principle is *preferable.* Since there are some arguments in favor of every

---

[1] Accounting Principles Board. "APB 20: Accounting Changes." July 1971 in *FASB Original Pronouncements,* Paragraph 15. Norwalk, CT: Financial Accounting Board.

accounting principle, the practical effect of the preferable requirement is that management must convince its auditors that the new principle is better. Auditors are required by GAAS to comment in their report on all changes in accounting principles, if they are material.

The auditing standard governing this comment states:

> *"If, however, there has been a change in accounting principles or in the method of their application that has a material effect on the comparability of the company's financial statements, the auditor should refer to the change in an explanatory paragraph of the report."*[2]

In other words, this standard requires the auditors to add an additional paragraph to their standard report. The same auditing standard provides the following example of an appropriate additional explanatory paragraph for an accounting change with which the auditors concur:

> *"As discussed in Note X to the financial statements, the Company changed its method of computing depreciation in 20X2."*[3]

If the auditors do *not* concur that a change in accounting principle is preferable, they are required take exception to the change as in the following example:

> *"Independent Auditor's Report*
> *[Same first and second paragraphs as the standard report]*
> *As disclosed in Note X to the financial statements, the Company adopted, in 20X2, the XYZ method of accounting, whereas it previously used the ABC method. Although use of the XYZ method is in conformity with accounting principles generally accepted in the United States of America, in our opinion the **Company has not provided reasonable justification for making this change,** as required by those principles.*
> *In our opinion, **except for the change in accounting principle discussed in the preceding paragraph,** the financial statements referred to above present fairly, in all material respects, the financial position of X*

---

[2] U.S. Auditing Standards, AU Section 508. "Reports On Auditing Financial Statements," paragraph 16. *http://www.pwccomperio.com/search97cgi/s97is_english.dll/search97cgi/ inetsrch_english.ini?action=formgen&Template=comperio.hts.* Accessed December 4, 2001.

[3] U.S. Auditing Standards, AU Section 508. "Reports On Auditing Financial Statements," paragraph 17. *http://www.pwccomperio.com/search97cgi/s97is_english.dll/search97cgi/ inetsrch_english.ini?action=formgen&Template=comperio.hts.* Accessed December 4, 2001.

Company as of December 31, 20X2 and 20X1, and the results of its operations and its cash flows for the years then ended in conformity with accounting principles generally accepted in the United States of America."[4] (emphasis added)

When auditors take exception to a change in accounting principle users of the financial statement will undoubtedly question management's motivation for making the change. This may cause an adverse stock price reaction.

COMMON CHANGES IN ACCOUNTING PRINCIPLES

Recent common changes in accounting principles have fallen into the following categories:

- **Revenue recognition policy.** Many industries have more than one method of recognizing revenue. A company may choose to change either to the predominant industry practice or to one that is less contentious with regulators or analysts.
- **Accounting for software development costs.** This might occur when a company changes how it determines which software construction costs are to be capitalized and which are R&D costs to be expensed.
- **Accounting for startup costs.** The AICPA has stated that:
  "Start-up activities are defined broadly as those one-time activities related to opening a new facility, introducing a new product or service, conducting business in a new territory, conducting business with a new class of customer or beneficiary, initiating a new process in an existing facility, or commencing some new operation. Start-up activities include activities related to organizing a new entity (commonly referred to as organization costs)."[5]

  A change in accounting for start-up costs occurs when a company changes from deferring and amortizing these costs to expensing them as incurred.
- **Accounting for business process reengineering costs.** Business process reengineering projects may consist of software development, software acquisition, software implementation, training, and ongoing support. Business process reengineering costs must be expensed, but some software costs can be capitalized. A company may change how it determines which costs fall into each category.

---

[4] Slightly modified example from U.S. Auditing Standards, AU Section 508. "Reports On Auditing Financial Statements," paragraph 52. *http://www.pwccomperio.com/search97cgi/ s97is_english.dll/search97cgi/inetsrch_english.ini?action=formgen&Template=comperio.h ts.* Accessed December 4, 2001.

[5] AICPA Accounting Standards Executive Committee. *Statement of Position 98-5 Reporting on the Costs of Start-Up Activities,* April 3, 1998, paragraph 5.

- **Valuing inventories.** A company may decide to switch from the Average Cost to the First-In-First-Out (FIFO) method of valuing inventory.
- **Computing depreciation.** A change from accelerated to straight-line depreciation will increase earnings because the amount of depreciation expense will be lower.

REPORTING CHANGES IN ACCOUNTING PRINCIPLES

GAAP require that most changes in accounting principle be reported by simply adopting the new method as of the first day of the current fiscal year so that the income statement for the current year will reflect use of the new method throughout the year.

The effect from adopting the principle for those years before the current fiscal year is computed and shown at the bottom of the current income statement, net of any tax effects, immediately before Net Income.

A few changes in accounting principles are so major that they would totally distort the current financial statements. GAAP provide that these changes be reported by retroactively restating all financial statements presented.

CASE STUDY: HERCULES INC. CHANGES TO NEW FASB STANDARD [6]

Hercules Incorporated is a diversified, worldwide producer of chemicals and related products that was incorporated in Delaware in 1912. As described in footnote 19 to its 1997 financial statement, Hercules changed its accounting principles due to new FASB requirements:

> *"Note 19. CHANGE IN ACCOUNTING PRINCIPLE*
>
> *In November 1997, FASB's Emerging Issues Task Force (EITF) reached a final consensus on Issue 97-13, "Accounting for Costs Incurred in Connection With a Consulting Contract That Combines Business Process Reengineering and Information Technology Transformation." Activities deemed to be business process reengineering include the following: current state assessments, configuring and prototyping, process reengineering, and work force restructuring. The consensus requires that the unamortized amounts of such costs previously capitalized as of the beginning of the quarter, which includes November 20, 1997, be charged during that quarter as the **cumulative effect of a change in accounting***

---

[6] *http://www.herc.com/shareholderinfo/annualreports/1997/page13.htm.* Accessed December 4, 2001; Hercules Incorporated 10-K for Fiscal Year Ending December 31, 1997. *http://www.sec.gov/Archives/edgar/data/46989/0000893220-98-000621.txt.* Accessed December 4, 2001.

principle. The company adopted the consensus during the fourth quarter of 1997 and *recorded a cumulative-effect adjustment of $5 million."* (emphasis added)

How Hercules recorded the $5 million cumulative effect of the change in accounting principle is shown in Figure 14.1.

Figure 14.1. Hercules Record of the Change in Accounting Principle

```
Consolidated Statement of Income (millions of dollars)
```

	Fiscal Year Ended December 31, 1997
Net sales	$1,866
Cost of sales	1,169
Selling, general, and administrative expenses	251
Research and development	53
Other operating expenses (income), net (Note 11)	165
Profit from operations	228
Equity in income of affiliated companies	30
Interest and debt expense (Note 12)	39
Other income, net (Note 13)	374
Income before income taxes and effect of change in accounting principle	593
Provision for income taxes (Note 14)	269
Income before effect of change in accounting principle	324
Effect of change in accounting principle (Note 19)	**(5)**
Net income	$319
Earnings before effect of change in accounting principle	$3.27
Effect	(0.05)
Earnings per share	$3.22

(emphasis added)

The Hercules auditors added a fourth paragraph to their report for 1997 because of the change in accounting principles:

"REPORT OF INDEPENDENT ACCOUNTANTS

To the Shareholders and the Board of Directors of Hercules Incorporated
Wilmington, Delaware

We have audited the accompanying consolidated balance sheets of Hercules Incorporated and subsidiary companies as of December 31, 1997 and 1996, and the related

*consolidated statements of income, stockholders' equi-
ty, and cash flow for each of the three years in the
period ended December 31, 1997. These financial statements are the responsibility of the company's management. Our responsibility is to express an opinion on
these financial statements based on our audits.*

*We conducted our audits in accordance with generally
accepted auditing standards. Those standards require
that we plan and perform the audit to obtain reasonable assurance about whether the financial statements
are free of material misstatement. An audit includes
examining, on a test basis, evidence supporting the
amounts and disclosures in the financial statements.
An audit also includes assessing the accounting principles used and significant estimates made by management, as well as evaluating the overall financial
statement presentation. We believe our audits provide
a reasonable basis for our opinion.*

*In our opinion, the financial statements referred to
above present fairly, in all material respects, the
consolidated financial position of Hercules
Incorporated and subsidiary companies as of December
31, 1997 and 1996, and the consolidated results of
their operations and cash flow for each of the three
years in the period ended December 31, 1997, in conformity with generally accepted accounting principles.*

**As discussed in Note 19 to the Financial Statements,
in 1997 the company changed its method of accounting
for costs incurred in connection with its enterprise
software installation.**

*Coopers & Lybrand L.L.P.
2400 Eleven Penn Center
Philadelphia, Pennsylvania 19103
February 13, 1998"*

"VOLUNTEERING" FOR A NEW ACCOUNTING STANDARD

Periodically the FASB, the GAAP rule-making body, adopts new accounting standards that either increase or decrease earnings when companies begin using them. Often, in order to ease the transition to a new standard, the FASB provides an "adoption window" of two to three years when companies can voluntarily adopt the new standard before it is actually required.

Voluntary early adoption of a new FASB standard may offer an opportunity to manage earnings. For example, it has been estimated that early adoption of Standard 52-Accounting for Foreign Currency Translation "gave the early adopting firms the opportunity to increase earnings an average of $ 0.38 per share, or about 11 percent of pre-change earnings."[7]

CASE STUDY: REYNOLDS METALS—VOLUNTARY ADOPTION OF A NEW FASB STANDARD[8]

Reynolds Metals Company, incorporated in Delaware in 1928, Reynolds serves global markets as a supplier and recycler of aluminum and other products, with its core business being as a vertically integrated producer of a wide variety of value-added aluminum products.

In 1993 Reynolds Metals had a $109 million operating loss. The company decided to voluntarily adopt the new GAAP for postretirement benefits; it resulted in an additional $610 million of after-tax expense, which, coupled with a $30 million accounting change for income taxes, increased its loss to $749 million. It described the accounting changes in two footnotes to its financial statement:

> "Note J
> IN 1992, **THE COMPANY ELECTED EARLY ADOPTION OF FAS NO. 106 – EMPLOYERS' ACCOUNTING FOR POSTRETIREMENT BENEFITS OTHER THAN PENSIONS.** FAS NO. 106 GENERALLY REQUIRES THE ACCRUAL OF THE EXPECTED COST OF POSTRE- TIREMENT BENEFITS (HEALTH CARE AND LIFE INSURANCE) BY THE DATE EMPLOYEES ATTAIN FULL ELIGIBILITY FOR BENE- FITS TO BE RECEIVED. PREVIOUSLY, THE EXPENSE FOR THESE BENEFITS WAS RECOGNIZED WHEN COSTS WERE INCURRED OR CLAIMS WERE RECEIVED.
>
> A charge of $610 million ($975 million before tax) was recognized in 1992 for the cumulative effects of this accounting change.

---

[7] Ayres, F. L. "Perceptions of Earnings Quality: What Managers Need To Know." *Management Accounting*, Vol. 76, No. 9, March, 1994, p. 36

[8] Reynolds Metals Co. 10-K for fiscal year ending December 31, 1994. *http://www.sec. gov/Archives/edgar/data/83604/0000083604-95-000006.txt*. Accessed December 04, 2001.

Note K - TAXES ON INCOME

IN 1992, THE COMPANY CHANGED ITS METHOD OF ACCOUNTING FOR INCOME TAXES FROM THE DEFERRED METHOD TO THE LIA-BILITY METHOD AS REQUIRED BY FAS NO. 109 - ACCOUNTING FOR INCOME TAXES. AS PERMITTED UNDER THE NEW RULES, PRIOR YEARS' FINANCIAL STATEMENTS HAVE NOT BEEN RESTATED.

A charge of $30 million was recognized in 1992 for the cumulative effects of this accounting change. Adoption of FAS No. 109 enabled full recognition of the deferred tax benefits associated with the adoption of FAS No. 106."

The effect of the accounting change is highlighted at the bottom of the income statements shown in Figure 14.2.

From the auditor's report it is clear that the auditors did not take exception to the accounting changes:

COMMON CHANGES IN ACCOUNTING ESTIMATES

The following types of changes in accounting estimates are fairly common:
- Uncollectible receivables.
- Inventory obsolescence.
- Useful lives and salvage value of assets.
- Period benefited by deferred costs.
- Liabilities for warranty costs and income taxes.
- Recoverable mineral reserves.[9]

Changes in accounting estimates are reported prospectively in the current and future period financial statements. No changes are made to past reported results or opening balances for the current period.

To illustrate, assume ABC Company's past practice has been to estimate uncollectible receivables as 3 percent of recorded sales revenue. The company decides to switch to estimating uncollectible receivables as a percentage of year-end receivables because this is the dominant method in its industry. This new method means that Uncollectible Accounts Expense will increase by $5 million, thereby decreasing Net Income by $5 million from what using the old method would have produced. ABC Company does not need to change any amounts reported in prior periods. It just needs to book the $5 million higher expense amount for the current year and, if it is material, disclose the details of the change in a footnote. In future years, it will just need to keep using the new method.

---

[9] Kieso, D. E., J. J. Weygandt, and T. D. Warfield. 2001. *Intermediate Accounting,* 10th ed. New York: John Wiley & Sons, Inc., p. 1263.

Figure 14.2. Effect of Accounting Change on Reynolds Income Statements

Consolidated Income Statements (In millions, except per
share amounts)

	1994	1993	1992
Net sales	$5,879.1	$5,269.2	$5,592.6
Equity, interest and other income	45.9	25.0	27.7
Gains on sales of assets	88.2	—	36.1
	6,013.2	5,294.2	5,656.4
Cost of products sold	5,278.5	4,930.3	5,031.8
Operational restructuring and asset revaluation costs	—	348.2	106.4
Selling, administrative and general expenses	389.0	371.6	382.8
Interest expense	155.6	159.2	166.8
Provision for estimated environmental costs	—	—	164.0
	5,823.1	5,809.3	5,851.8
Income (loss) before income taxes and cumulative effects of accounting changes	190.1	(515.1)	(195.4)
Taxes on income (credit)	68.4	(193.0)	(86.2)
Income (loss) before cumulative effects of accounting changes	121.7	(322.1)	(109.2)
Cumulative effects of accounting changes (1)	—	—	(639.6)
Net income (loss)	$121.7	$(322.1)	$(748.8)

(emphasis added)

"REPORT OF ERNST & YOUNG LLP, INDEPENDENT AUDITORS

Stockholders and Board of Directors
Reynolds Metals Company

*We have audited the accompanying consolidated balance
sheets of Reynolds Metals Company as of December 31,
1994 and 1993, and the related consolidated statements
of income and retained earnings, and cash flows for
each of the three years in the period ended December
31, 1994.*

*These financial statements are the responsibility of
the Company's management. Our responsibility is to
express an opinion on these financial statements based
on our audits.*

*We conducted our audits in accordance with generally
accepted auditing standards. Those standards require
that we plan and perform the audit to obtain reason-*

Figure 14.2. Effect of Accounting Change on Reynolds Income Statements, *Cont'd*

> *able assurance about whether the financial statements are free of material misstatement. An audit includes examining, on a test basis, evidence supporting the amounts and disclosures in the financial statements. An audit also includes assessing the accounting principles used and significant estimates made by management, as well as evaluating the overall financial statement presentation. We believe that our audits provide a reasonable basis for our opinion.*
>
> *In our opinion, the financial statements referred to above present fairly, in all material respects, the consolidated financial position of Reynolds Metals Company at December 31, 1994 and 1993, and the consolidated results of its operations and its cash flows for each of the three years in the period ended December 31, 1994, in conformity with generally accepted accounting principles.*
>
> **As discussed in the notes to the consolidated financial statements, the Company changed its methods of accounting for postretirement benefits other than pensions (Note J)** *and income taxes (Note K) in 1992.*
>
> *Ernst & Young LLP*
> *Richmond, Virginia*
> *February 17, 1995"*
>
> (emphasis added)

CHANGE IN REPORTING ENTITY

Because GAAP requirements for changing the reporting entity were discussed in the previous chapter, they will not be repeated here. The rules apply to:

- *Acquisition of subsidiaries.*
- *Disposition of subsidiaries.*
- *Change in the cost, equity, or consolidation methods of accounting for subsidiaries or investment.*

15 METHODS OF WRITING-OFF LONG-TERM ASSETS

There are numerous assumptions and methods used for writing off long-term assets. This chapter explains how to choose the most appropriate.

For many companies a very large portion of the balance sheet is comprised on long-term assets that are subject to write-off. The process of writing off assets transfers their value from their asset category in the balance sheet to an expense in the income statement.

Most executives are surprised at how much judgment is involved in selecting the methods and assumptions that are behind these write-offs. Since the bottom line is directly affected, making these judgments offers an opportunity for earnings management.

LONG-TERM ASSET CATEGORIES

The three principal categories of long-term assets and the related general write-off methods are shown in Table 15.1.

MAJOR MANAGEMENT JUDGMENTS

The basic purpose behind writing off long-lived assets is to match the decline in their usefulness with the periods benefited—in other words, to transfer a portion of the asset cost from the balance sheet to the income statement as the asset is used to produce revenues.

Table 15.1. How Assets Are Written Off

Asset Category	Items in Category	Write-Off Method
Property, plant, and equipment	Land, buildings, machinery, tools	Depreciation
Natural resources	Oil, natural gas, coal, timber	Depletion
Intangibles	Patents, copyrights, trademarks	Amortization

The write-off process is a process not of valuation but of cost allocation. Assets are recorded in the balance sheet at cost when acquired and carried in the balance sheet at cost minus any write-offs already transferred to the balance sheet.

Asset valuation enters into the write-off picture only when an asset is considered impaired. A special write-off due to impairment has already been discussed in the chapter on big bath write-offs.

Management has discretion to make the following judgments about long-lived assets:

- Write-off method—slow or fast?
- Write-off period—long or short?
- Salvage value estimation—high or low?
- Change to non-operating use: discontinue the write-off of the asset cost.

WRITE-OFF METHODS

The accounting literature discusses a large number of write-off methods but they can generally be classified into just three categories:

1. *Straight-line write-offs* include all methods that provide a constant or even annual write-off. Management would choose these methods to minimize expenses and thus maximize income. These are the choice of the vast majority of companies.

2. *Accelerated write-offs* include all methods that provide for a larger write-off in the initial years of an asset's life and a smaller write-off in the later years. Management would choose one of these methods to maximize expenses so as to minimize income. Many companies use accelerated write-offs for income tax reporting; tax law allows companies to use different methods on their tax returns than they use on their publicly reported financial statements.

3. *Units-of-production write-offs* include all methods that provide a write-off that varies according to how much of an asset was used. Management would choose these methods to match expense with income generated from the asset.

The difference between the first two methods can be illustrated by this example: Assume a machine is bought for $15,000. Its useful life is estimated to be five years, at the end of which it will have zero value. Table 15.2 illustrates the difference between using the most common straight-line method for this asset and an accelerated write-off method called "sum-of-the-years digits."

Table 15.2. Straight-Line and Accelerated Depreciation Compared

Method	Year 1	Year 2	Year 3	Year 4	Year 5	Total Write-Off Over 5 Years
Straight-line	$3,000	$3,000	$3,000	$3,000	$3,000	$15,000
Accelerated (sum-of-the-years digits)	$5,000	$4,000	$3,000	$2,000	$ 1,000	$15,000

The data in the previous table may be seen from a different angle in Figure 15.1.

Figure 15.1. Comparison of Straight-line Versus Accelerated Write-Off

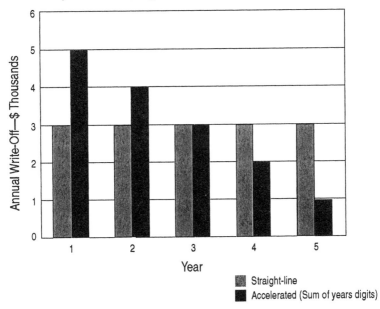

As you can see, both methods write off exactly the same total amount—$15,000. The difference is that the accelerated method is front-end-loaded.

Earnings management could come into play in a situation where a company was expecting an increase in earnings that it did not think it could sustain over time. By using an accelerated depreciation method for long-term asset additions, it could claim a higher expense, which would dampen earnings for a few years. There are numerous theoretical arguments for taking accelerated depreciation, so adoption of accelerated depreciation for new acquisitions should not be difficult to justify under GAAP.

CASE STUDY: DUPONT SWITCHES TO STRAIGHT-LINE WRITE-OFF[1]

The following was taken from DuPont's fiscal year 1995 10-K report:

> *"DuPont was founded in 1802 and incorporated in Delaware in 1915. The company is one of the leading chemical producers worldwide and the largest in the United States.* **The company conducts fully integrated petroleum operations through its wholly owned subsidiary, Conoco Inc.** *In 1994, it ranked eighth in the worldwide production of petroleum liquids by U.S.- based companies, tenth in the production of natural gas, and sixth in refining capacity."* (emphasis added)

For the fiscal year ending December 31, 1995, Dupont reported revenues of $42,163 million and net income of $3,293 million. Total assets were $37,312 million. Depreciation, depletion, and amortization expense was $2,722 million—83 percent of net income for the year.

In 1995, Dupont changed from accelerated to straight-line depreciation. This caused an estimated $250 million[2] decrease in depreciation expense for the year. Because management and the auditors considered the change immaterial (too small an effect to be significant), the effect of the change was neither disclosed separately in the income statement nor mentioned in the audit report. The following footnote is the only information that was provided about the accounting change:

> *"Property, Plant and Equipment*
>
> *Property, plant and equipment (PP&E) is carried at cost and, except for petroleum PP&E, PP&E placed in service prior to 1995 is depreciated under the sum-of-the-years' digits method and other substantially similar methods. PP&E placed in service after 1994 is depreciated using the straight-line method.* **This change in accounting was made to reflect management's**

---

[1] E. I. DuPont De Nemours and Company 10-K for Fiscal Year Ending December 31, 1995. *http://www.sec.gov/Archives/edgar/data/30554/0000950109-96-001642.txt.* Accessed December 7, 2001.

[2] Kieso, D.E., J. J. Weygandt, and T. D. Warfield. 2001. *Intermediate Accounting,* 10th ed. New York: John Wiley & Sons, Inc., p. 558.

belief that the productivity of such PP&E will not appreciably diminish in the early years of its useful life, and it will not be subject to significant additional maintenance in the later years of its useful life. **In these circumstances, straight-line depreciation is preferable** in that it provides a better matching of costs with revenues. Additionally, the change to the straight-line method conforms to predominant industry practice. The effect of this change on net income will be dependent on the level of future capital spending; **it did not have a material effect in 1995.** " (emphasis added)

But what was the effect of the switch to straight-line depreciation on the earnings DuPont would report in the following years? The answer is that DuPont would report less depreciation expense and higher earnings as a result of having made the accounting change.

WRITE-OFF PERIODS

Long-term asset write-offs are based on the estimated useful life of the asset. The useful life and the physical life are not necessarily the same. A personal computer may be physically capable of running without major repair for 20 years, but its useful life may be only three to five years because newer, more efficient and economical computers are likely to become available, making it obsolete.

A long-term asset's useful life may also be shorter than its physical life if it becomes inadequate to the task at hand—for example, if the company grows very rapidly and the computer simply cannot handle the volume of processing tasks for the larger organization.

The time over which a long-term asset is written off is typically selected in one of the following ways:

- A company's past experience with the same or a similar asset.
- Engineering estimates.
- Manufacturer's data suggesting asset useful life or "mean time to failure."
- Guideline lives for similar assets based on industry wide studies.

The past need not control the future when a long-term asset write-off period is selected. If the future is expected to be different from past experience, a company may be justified in writing off long-term assets over a different period than was used for past assets. For example, management may decide that the pace of innovation in personal computers has slowed and that it would now be appropriate to write them off over five years even though in the past experience the company deemed them obsolete and replaced them every three years.

Often write-off periods are given as ranges rather than exact terms. For example, if the guideline life range for a computer-controlled milling machine is five to eight years, management would normally be justified in selecting any life within this range.

CASE STUDY: BOISE CASCADE—ESTIMATED USEFUL LIFE[3]

Boise Cascade Corporation is a major distributor of office products and building materials; it manufactures and distributes paper and wood products. In 2000, the company had approximately $2,873 million in long-term assets in the property plant and equipment category on its balance sheet—55 percent of the $5,267 million in reported total assets. The company used a variety of write-off methods and lives for these assets. The information shown in Figure 15.2 was taken from the fiscal year 2000 Boise Cascade 10-K report.

Figure 15.2. Boise Cascade 2000 Balance Sheet Showing Write-Off Methods

```
                          BALANCE SHEET
              Boise Cascade Corporation and Subsidiaries
                                            December 31, 2000
ASSETS                                         (thousands)
Current
  Cash and cash equivalents                 $      62,820
  Receivables, less allowances of $7,607,000
    and $11,289,000                                671,793
  Inventories                                      747,829
  Deferred income tax benefits                      50,924
  Other                                             43,955
                                                 1,577,321
Property
  Property and equipment
    Land and land improvements                      70,551
    Buildings and improvements                     648,256
    Machinery and equipment                      4,447,628
                                                 5,166,435
  Accumulated depreciation                      (2,584,784)
                                                 2,581,651
  Timber, timberlands, and timber deposits         291,132
                                                 2,872,783
Goodwill, net of amortization of $49,053,000
  and $52,506,000                                  403,331
Investments in equity affiliates                   134,757
Other assets                                       278,731
Total assets                                    $5,266,923
```

[3] Boise Cascade Corporation 10K for Fiscal Year 2000. *http://www.sec.gov/Archives/edgar/data/12978/000001297801500005/ss01231o.htm.* Accessed December 7, 2001.

Figure 15.2. Boise Cascade 2000 Balance Sheet Showing Write-Off Methods, *Cont'd*

Property. Property and equipment are recorded at cost. Cost includes expenditures for major improvements and replacements and the net amount of interest cost associated with significant capital additions. Capitalized interest was $1,458,000 in 2000, $238,000 in 1999, and $1,341,000 in 1998. Most of our paper and wood products manufacturing facilities determine depreciation by the **units-of-production method**. Other operations use the **straight-line method**. Gains and losses from sales and retirements are included in income as they occur.

Depreciation is computed over the following estimated useful lives:

Buildings and improvements	5 to 40 years
Furniture and fixtures	**5 to 10 years**
Machinery, equipment, and delivery trucks	3 to 20 years
Leasehold improvements	5 to 10 years[4]

(emphasis added)

The options chosen by Boise Cascade demonstrate that a company may have a fairly wide range of estimated useful lives for different categories of assets.

ESTIMATING SALVAGE VALUE

Some, though not all, long-term asset write-off methods incorporate salvage values in their computations, which changes the amount of annual write-off. Assume that a $15,000 machine with an estimated five-year life will have a salvage value estimated to range from $2,500 to $5,000. The annual write-off can be computed using both ends of the range, $2,500 and $5,000 as shown in Table 15.3.

Clearly, the higher the salvage value, the lower the annual write-off. If any value within the range of salvage values is equally plausible, managers are justified in selecting any value in the range.

Table 15.3. Salvage Value Estimates

Method	Year 1	Year 2	Year 3	Year 4	Year 5	Total Write-Off Over 5 Years
Straight-line with $2,500 salvage value ([$15,000-$2,500]/5 years) = $2,500	$2,500	$2,500	$2,500	$2,500	$2,500	$12,500
Straight-line with $5,000 salvage value ([$15,000-$5,000]/5 years) = $2,000	$2,000	$2,000	$2,000	$2,000	$2,000	$10,000

---

[4] Ibid.

CHANGE TO NON-OPERATING USE

Management may decide to idle certain production facilities for an extended period, perhaps due to a business slowdown or while seeking a purchaser.

Long-term assets not currently employed in production are considered *non-operating assets*. They should be segregated from operating assets in the balance sheet and all annual write-offs discontinued, whether these are calculated by depreciation, depletion, or amortization. There would be no write-off for these assets unless they meet the impairment criteria discussed earlier.

16 SALE/LEASEBACK AND ASSET EXCHANGE TECHNIQUES

This chapter explains basic lease accounting to set the stage for describing sale/ leaseback transactions as a way to manage earnings.

Timely disposition of long-term productive assets that are carried in the balance sheet at historical cost can make it possible to record unrealized gains or losses. Two methods used to accomplish this are:

1. *Outright sale.* A company can sell a long-term asset that has unrealized gains or losses in a year when earnings need a gain or loss. Suppose the corporation owns a building that is carried in the balance sheet at $30,000,000 but is really worth $50,000,000. If the building is sold, the corporation can book a $20,000,000 gain to boost current period earnings. (Of course, there are also operational and tax considerations to take into account.)

2. *Sale/leaseback.* In a sale/leaseback, one company sells an asset to another, which immediately leases it back to the seller. GAAP has detailed rules about whether a lease qualifies as a *capital lease* (considered equivalent to retaining ownership) or an *operating lease* (equivalent to merely renting the property). Though losses occurring in a sale/leaseback transaction are recognized immediately on the seller's books, gains are deferred and amortized into income, over the life of the of the asset if it is a capital lease or in proportion to the rental payments if it is an operating lease.

It is also possible to dispose of long-term productive assets without recording *any* gain or loss. This is achieved by exchange of similar productive assets:

> *When companies exchange similar productive assets, paragraph 21(b) of APB 29 allows an exception to the general rule of recording a gain or loss on disposal of long-term assets.*

LEASING

Many companies finance or "rent" a large portion of their operating assets via lease agreements because of the many advantages of leasing compared with actually owning assets. When a company has use of assets for operations but does not have to report either the asset or the lease liability in the corporate balance sheet, this is called "off-balance sheet" financing.

In 1964 the accounting profession implemented an opinion that set the stage for some extremely complex rules for accounting for lease transactions.[1] The purpose was to prevent leasing from being used as a mechanism to implement off-balance sheet financing where the economic substance was that the lessee really had significant ownership rights. These rules are now so complex that they are almost incomprehensible. Nevertheless, this chapter briefly explains the basic nature of these rules and then discusses sale/leaseback transactions as a way of managing earnings.

LEASING ADVANTAGES

A *lessee* is a company that signs a written agreement promising to make payments to another company for use of an asset. A *lessor* is the company that provides the asset in exchange for the lease payments. Typically, the lessor retains legal title to the asset throughout the term of the lease. Leases can get quite complicated in situations when third parties finance the lease transaction.

Although leasing can have disadvantages, such as being locked into a long-term contract or high financing costs, the following potential advantages for a lessee have contributed to growth of leasing over time in our economy:

- *No down payments.* Leases rarely require any down payments, so the lessee can preserve cash.

- *Obsolescence protection.* Leases frequently provide that the leased asset is to be returned to the lessor at the expiration of the lease term, thus protecting the lessee from owning equipment or other assets that have become less useful or obsolete.

---

[1] Accounting Principles Board Opinion Number 5. *Reporting of Leases in the Financial Statements of Lessee.* http://www.pwccomperio.com/search97cgi/s97is_english.dll/ search97cgi/ inetsrch_english.ini?action=formgen&Template=comperio.hts. Accessed December 11, 2001.

- *Lower cost and flexible financing.* Lease terms may cost less than traditional financing because the lessor has operating economies of scale or can use tax benefits more fully. Moreover, lease payment terms can be structured to meet the lessee's cash flow schedule.
- *Off-balance sheet financing.* Leases can be structured so that they do not have to be reported on the balance sheet, so that assets and debt can be omitted from the balance sheet. This may result in a better debt-to-equity or asset turnover ratio. However, an early study found no significant effect on stock or bond prices when leases *were* reported on the balance sheet.[2]

LESSEE ACCOUNTING

The GAAP accounting rules require that a lessee record a lease as either an operating or a capital lease. Lessees would generally prefer that the lease qualify as operating to avoid reporting it on the balance sheet. An operating lease is defined by default as any lease that does not meet the criteria for a capital lease. A non-cancelable lease that meets *any one* of the following four criteria qualifies, and must be recorded, as a capital lease:[3]

1. *Lease transferring ownership.* This criterion is met if the lease agreement transfers title of the asset to the lessee. For example, a five-year car lease might transfer title to the lessee upon the last lease payment.
2. *Bargain purchase option.* A lease option that lets the lessee buy the property for an amount that is significantly lower than the fair market value of the property at the date the option becomes exercisable is considered a "bargain purchase" option. A five-year car lease that transfers title to the lessee for $1 upon the last lease payment would meet this criterion.
3. *Lease term equalling or exceeding 75 percent of asset's economic life.* A lease that covers a substantial portion of the asset's economic life is considered to be a capital lease. A five-year lease for a car with an expected useful economic life of six years would meet this criterion (6 years x 75% = 4.5 years).
4. *Present value of lease payments equalling or exceeding 90 percent of asset's fair market value.* If the discounted value of the lease payments is approximately equal to the asset's fair value, it would be a capital lease. Assume a car has a fair market value of $20,000. A five-year lease

---

[2] Abdel-Khalik, A. R. "The Economic Effects on Lessees of FASB Statement No. 13, Accounting For Leases." Research Report. Stamford, CT: FASB, 1981.
[3] Kieso, D. E., J. J. Weygandt, and T. D. Warfield. 2001. *Intermediate Accounting,* 10th ed. New York: John Wiley & Sons, Inc., pp. 1190-1198.

with 60 monthly payments of $400 would meet this criterion if the interest rate were 6 percent (present value of 60 payments of $400 at 6% = $20,690.92).

For an operating lease, the accounting is fairly simple. The lessee simply charges the lease payments to an operating expense category in the income statement and nothing is recorded in the balance sheet. For example, with a two-year operating lease for a building at $5,000 per month, the lessee would record a monthly rent expense of $5,000 in the income statement. Nothing would appear in the lessee's balance sheet relative to the lease.

Capital lease requirements are considerably more complex because the lessee must record the lease as if an asset had been purchased and financed with a debt agreement. This means that, at the time the lease agreement is signed, the lessee company will record both an asset and a liability in the balance sheet. Every month for the term of the lease, it will then record both depreciation expense on the asset and interest expense on the liability.

To illustrate a capital lease, assume that a company entered into a 10-year non-cancelable agreement to lease a building with an estimated fair market value of $300,000 at $5,000 per month. The company's borrowing cost was 10 percent in annual interest. The present value at 10 percent annual interest on 120 monthly payment of $5,000 is $378,356. The lessee would have to record in its balance sheet a Leased Building as an asset worth $378,356 and a liability for the Capital Lease Obligation for $378, 356 in its balance sheet.[4] The lessee would then continue to record depreciation expense on the asset and interest expense on the liability.

LESSOR ACCOUNTING

Lessors are required by GAAPto record leases as either operating or as one of two types of capital leases. If reimbursable costs are reasonably estimable and collection of the lease payments is reasonably assured, exactly the same four criteria that apply in classifying capital leases for lessees apply for lessors. Each type has a different accounting treatment as explained next.

1. *Operating.* Lease payments received are recorded as rental revenues and the leased asset is retained in balance sheet and depreciated. The leased asset remains in the lessor's balance sheet.

2. *Direct financing.* The leased asset is removed from the balance sheet and replaced with an asset, Lease Receivable. In addition to the assets cost, the Lease Receivable account is also increased for unearned interest revenue over the life of the lease. Each lease payment received is record-

---

[4] The lease qualifies as a capital lease because the $378,356 present value of the lease payments exceeds 90 percent of the building's $300,000 fair market value.

ed as a reduction in the account, which is also reduced for Interest Revenue earned over the life of the lease.

Assume that a company leased a building with a book and fair market value of $378,400 at $5,000 per month on a 10-year noncancelable lease with the company's rate of return being 10 percent. At 10 percent annual interest, the present value of 120 monthly payment of $5,000 is $378,356.

The lessor would remove the $378,400 building from its balance sheet and transfer $378,400 to the asset account, Lease Receivable, which would also be increased by $221,600 for the unearned interest implicit in the lease agreement ($600,000 of lease payments - $378,400 building fair market value = $221,600 implicit interest). The total in the Lease Receivable would then be $600,000.

As the lessor receives the $5,000 lease payment each month, it records a $5,000 reduction in the Lease Receivable account and also records monthly Interest Revenue in a way that would result in all the $221,600 of implicit interest being recognized over the 10-year lease term.

With this method, the leased asset is removed from the lessor's balance sheet but replaced by a lease receivable.

3. *Sales-type.* A sales-type lease is like a direct financing lease but it has an element of manufacturer's or dealer's profit incorporated into it. This means the cost of the asset leased does not equal the present value of the lease payments. This profit element is recognized at the point the lease is signed.

Assume that a company leases equipment with a book value of $300,000 at $5,000 per month on a 10-year noncancelable lease agreement with a rate of return of 10 percent. Since the present value at 10 percent annual interest of 120 monthly payments of $5,000 is $378,356, the fair market value of the equipment is presumed to be $378,356, and the profit would be the amount above book value.

At the time the lease is signed, the lessor would remove the $300,000 cost for equipment from its balance sheet and transfer that $300,000 plus a profit element of $78,356 to an asset account, Lease Receivable. The lessor would also at that time recognize $78,356 of revenue in the income statement. The Lease Receivable account would be increased for the $221,600 of unearned interest implicit in the lease agreement, bringing the balance in the account to $600,000, the $378,400 fair market value of the equipment and the $221,600 implicit interest. The lessor would then proceed to record the monthly $5,000 lease payments just it would if this were a direct financing lease.

With this method, the leased asset is again removed from the lessor's balance sheet and replaced by a lease receivable, but the lessor must also record a profit from the sale of the leased item at the time the lease is signed.

SALE/LEASEBACKS

A sale/leaseback occurs whenever a company sells an asset to another party and then immediately leases it back. Whiting describes this type of transaction in more detail:

> *"What is a sale-leaseback? Essentially, it involves the sale of a corporate headquarters, distribution facility, manufacturing facility, laboratory, or other physical property that will continue to be used by the seller. The divested asset can include a specific property in a single location or multiple properties in a number of locations. If the property is under construction or is about to be constructed, the sale-leaseback can be structured to provide a 'take-out' on completion, or in some cases to actually fund the project while it is being constructed.*
>
> *As part of the arrangement, the former corporate owner leases the facility back from the purchaser for a period of time—typically 10 to 25 years—and the seller retains control of the property. Many sale-leasebacks are structured as 'triple net,' meaning that the seller/lessee remains responsible for all operating expenses, insurance, taxes, and maintenance of the property."[5]*

There are several possible business reasons for entering into this type of transaction:[6]

- *Obtain working capital.* The company selling the asset usually receives cash from the sale , thus obtaining working capital while retaining use of the asset. More companies are now taking advantage of this technique:

> *"Sale-lease-backs have been around for decades. But more and more corporations are recognizing that cash tied up in real estate can be more effectively deployed in their core businesses and are accelerating the use of sale-lease-back financing to monetize bricks and mortar."[7]*

Some years ago, for instance, *Reader's Digest* realigned its use of capital in an attempt to better maximize shareholder value:

> *"The Reader's Digest Association, Inc. has successfully completed the $96 million sale of its U.K. company's headquarters building at 11 Westferry Circus, Canary Wharf in London's Docklands, to DIFA, one of Germany's largest open ended property funds. Reader's Digest in turn,*

---

[5] Whiting, G. J. "Monetize Your Bricks and Mortar Through a Sale-Leaseback." *Mergers & Acquisitions,* November-December 1999. *http://www.findarticles.com/cf_dls/m6402/3_34/58065173/p1/article.jhtml.* Accessed December 12, 2001.
[6] Kieso, et al., op. cit., n. 3, p. 1228.
[7] Whiting, op. cit., n. 5.

will enter into a long-term lease with DIFA to occupy about two-thirds of the building. Reader's Digest is one of a growing number of corporations that are selling off their real estate holdings in order to generate shareholder value."[8]

- **Refinance.** If the asset was originally financed and interest rates have since dropped, a sale/leaseback can allow a company to take advantage of the lower interest rates. Alternatively, it may simply be that the lessor can finance the property much more cheaply than the lessee:

  "The buyer is often an established institutional entity, such as a real estate investment trust, partnership, or limited liability corporation, that has access to capital on more attractive terms than the corporation may be able to obtain independently. This is especially important when the target company is being recapitalized or restructured."[9]

- **Tax benefits.** If ownership of the property might affect a company's minimum tax liability, divestiture of ownership might resolve this potential problem.

A sale/leaseback may generate either an immediate loss or a deferred profit, depending on the circumstances. We will look at the GAAP loss rules first.

If the fair market value of the leased asset is less than the book value, a loss must be immediately recognized for the full amount. For example, if Company A sells and then leases back equipment that has a book value of $30 million but a fair market value of only $20 million, it will record an immediate $10 million loss—the company can thus manage earnings by unlocking the unrecognized losses in a sale/leaseback. If the fair value of the leased asset is more than the book value, a deferred gain is generated. If the lease meets any of the criteria for a capital lease, this gain is taken into income at the same rate as the asset is depreciated. If the lease meets the criteria for an operating lease, the gain is taken into income in proportion to the rental payments. For example, if Company A sells and then leases back on a 10 year lease equipment with a book value of $30 million but a fair market value of $40 million, it will record a $10 million deferred gain. Using straight-line depreciation and with annual lease payments being equal, the gain would be taken into income at the rate of $1 million per year for the 10 years of the lease. Once again, the company can manage earnings, this time by unlocking unrealized gains!

The beauty of both these approaches is that the company generates a recordable gain or loss while retaining use of the leased asset.

---

[8] *Realty Times,* February 15, 1999. *http://realtytimes.com/rtnews/rtcpages/19990215_rupreaddigest.htm.* Accessed December 13, 2001.

[9] Whiting, op. cit., n. 5.

CASE STUDY: ETEC—BUILDING SALE/LEASEBACK¹⁰

Etec is a high technology company. In the fiscal year ending July 31, 1995, it had revenues of $82,916,000 and net income of $6,844,000. During that year Etec sold and then leased back its principal building, recording a $7 million deferred gain on the transaction. In accordance with GAAP, this gain is being amortized and taken into income over the 15 years of the lease.

An interesting wrinkle in this transaction was that Etec issued warrants on its common stock to the lessor. These warrants were apparently a "sweetener" to give the lessor additional compensation.

The ETEC sale/leaseback is described in more detail in the following paragraphs taken from the company's financial statements:

> *"Etec Systems, Inc. ("Etec" or the "Company") is a world leader in the production of mask pattern generation equipment for the semiconductor industry. Etec designs, develops, manufactures and markets equipment that produces high precision masks, which are used to print circuit patterns onto semiconductor wafers. Etec sells its MEBES electron beam systems and its CORE and ALTA laser beam systems at prices currently ranging from approximately $3.2 million to $7.3 million each and accessories and upgrades at prices currently ranging from less than $400,000 to $3.0 million each.*
>
> *NOTE 12—COMMITMENTS AND CONTINGENCIES:*
>
> *In February 1995, the Company entered into a sale and leaseback agreement, pursuant to which the Company sold its office/manufacturing facilities (the "Property") located in Hayward, California for approximately $11.8 million and leased back the Property for an initial term of fifteen years, with options for four five-year renewals. Initial annual rental payments to the lessor are approximately $1.4 million for the first three years. At the end of the third, sixth, ninth and twelfth years, respectively, the rent will be adjusted by an amount based on*

---

¹⁰ ETEC 10-K for Fiscal Year 1996 10-K. h*ttp://www.sec.gov/Archives/edgar/data/851397/ 0000950109-96-007013.txt.* Accessed December 13, 2001.

any percentage increase in the Consumer Price Index for the preceding three years, with a cap of 12%. Under the terms of the lease, the Company is responsible for paying maintenance, insurance, taxes, and all other expenses associated with operating and maintaining the Property. **The Company recorded the transaction as a sale and deferred the gain on the sale that was approximately $7.0 million. This gain is being amortized over the 15-year operating lease term.**

NOTE 6—STOCKHOLDERS' EQUITY:

In February 1995, **in conjunction with entering into a sale and leaseback agreement** *(Note 12),* **the Company issued the lessor a warrant** *to purchase 159,314 shares of the Company's Common Stock at $0.45 per share. Additionally, the Company issued to the bank providing mortgage financing to the lessor a warrant to purchase 53,104 shares of Common Stock at $0.45 per share. These warrants expire on November 15, 2003.* **The value assigned to these warrants is being amortized over the lease period, which is 15 years,** *and is not material."* (emphasis added)

CASE STUDY: ADVANCED MICRO DEVICES— SALE/LEASEBACK OF CORPORATE HEADQUARTERS[11]

Advanced Micro Devices, Inc. is a semiconductor manufacturer with manufacturing and sales facilities throughout the world. In fiscal year 1998 the company recorded revenues of $2,542 million and a net loss of $104 million. As noted in the footnotes, Advanced Micro Devices recorded a deferred gain of $34 million from a sale/ leaseback of its corporate headquarters.

> *"Included in Other is a deferred gain of $34 million recorded during 1998 as a result of the sale and leaseback of our corporate marketing, general and administrative facility. The deferred gain will be amortized over the lease term, which is 20 years (see Note 12).*

---

[11] Advanced Micro Devices 10-K for Fiscal Year Ended December 27, 1998. *http://www.sec. gov/Archives/edgar/data/2488/0001012870-99-000892.txt.* Accessed December 13, 2001.

> *The operating lease of our corporate marketing, general and adminis-*
> *trative facility expired in December 1998. At the end of the lease term,*
> *we were obligated to either purchase the facility or to arrange for its*
> *sale to a third party with a guarantee of residual value to the seller*
> *equal to the option purchase price. In December 1998, we arranged for*
> *the sale of the facility to a third party and leased it back under a new*
> *operating lease. We realized a gain of $34 million as a part of this trans-*
> *action. We have deferred the gain and will amortize it over a period of*
> *20 years, the life of the lease."*

The deferred gain will increase income for Advanced Micro Devices in future accounting periods.

EXCHANGE OF SIMILAR PRODUCTIVE ASSETS

A company can exchange (swap) a long-term productive asset for a similar asset without having to record any gain or loss because the exchange is not viewed as the "culmination of an earnings process." This treatment is described as follows:

> *"Opinion 29 includes an exception to the basic principle of fair value*
> *for transactions in which an enterprise exchanges a productive asset for*
> *a similar productive asset or an equivalent interest in the same or simi-*
> *lar productive asset (the similar productive asset exception). The Board*
> *concluded that such an exchange was **not essentially the culmination of***
> ***an earnings process.***
>
>   *A **productive asset** is defined in paragraph 3(e) of Opinion 29 as*
> *'assets held for or used in the production of goods or services by the*
> *enterprise. Productive assets include an investment in another entity if*
> *the investment is accounted for by the equity method but exclude an*
> *investment not accounted for by that method.' Paragraph 3(e) of Opinion*
> *29 defines **similar productive assets** as 'productive assets that are of the*
> *same general type, that perform the same function or that are employed*
> *in the same line of business.' "[12]* (emphasis added)

Examples of productive assets are provided in APB 29, Paragraph 7(c):

> *"(c) exchange of productive assets-assets employed in production rather*
> *than held for sale in the ordinary course of business—for similar pro-*
> *ductive assets or for an equivalent interest in similar productive assets.*
> *Examples of exchanges in category (c) include the trade of player con-*
> *tracts by professional sports organizations, exchange of leases on miner-*

---

[12] EITF 01-2 Interpretations of APB 29. h*ttp://www.pwccomperio.com/search97cgi/s97is_english.dll/search97cgi/inetsrch_english.ini?action=formgen&Template=comperio.hts.* Accessed June 25, 2003.

al properties, exchange of one form of interest in an oil producing prop-erty for another form of interest, exchange of real estate for real estate. "[13]

Note that a productive asset can be stock in a company if that investment is accounted for under the equity method. Generally the equity method is employed for stock ownerships percentages in the range of 20 to 50 percent. This means that qualifying subsidiaries may be disposed of with no gain or loss recorded.

[13] APB 29, Accounting for Nonmonetary Transactions, Paragraph 7 (c).
http://www.pwccomperio.com/search97cgi/s97is_english.dll/search97cgi/inetsrch_english.ini?action=formgen&Template=comperio.hts. Accessed June 25, 2003.

17 ABOVE THE LINE OR BELOW THE LINE?

This chapter discusses the significance of where items are reported in the income statement. Whether items are classified under operating or non-operating income may affect corporate share valuation.

Core (permanent) earnings are those that are expected to continue into the future. Noncore (transitory or value-irrelevant) earnings are nonrecurring earnings. Financial analysts and other financial statement users typically project growth rates for core earnings and then discount future core earnings back to the present to estimate the value of a stock. Thus, it is important that they be able to determine which earnings components in the income statement are core and which are not.

GAAPspecifies how items are to be reported in the income statement in order to facilitate forecasting core earnings. This is done by first reporting operating items and computing operating income. Nonoperating income items are then reported after operating income. Those components making up operating income are considered to be "above the line" representing operating income. Those items that are not part of operating income are reported after it or "below the line."

INCOME STATEMENT CATEGORIES

There are four possible income statement categories for reporting unusual items not considered part of normal operating income:

1. *Special or unusual charges.* Unusual items that management wants to report separately from regular operating items may not be presented net of tax effects and must be reported in operating income even though they may be separately disclosed.

2. *Discontinued operations.* Business operations that have been sold or closed.

3. *Extraordinary gains and losses.* Items considered both unusual and infrequent.

4. *Cumulative effect of change in accounting principles.* The income effect on prior years of changes in accounting principles during the current year.

The last three items must be presented net of any income tax effects so that the effect of these items on the company may be easily removed from net income when core earnings are computed.

GAAP assign each of these categories a precise location in the income statement. The locations are fixed so that there is no question about the nature and interpretation of the items. The previously discussed four categories are numbered in the stylized income statement shown in Figure 17.1.

Figure 17.1. Reporting of Unusual Items on the Income Statement

XYZ Company
Income Statement
For the year ended December 31, 20X4

Revenue	$xxx
Cost of goods sold	xxx
Gross profit	xxx
Selling, general and administrative expenses	xxx
Income from operations	xxx
Other revenue and gains	
Interest revenue	xxx
Other expenses and losses	
Interest expense	xxx
[1] *UNUSUAL CHARGE-LOSS ON INVENTORY WRITEDOWN*	*xxx*
Income from continuing operations before income tax	xxx
Income tax	xxx
["The Line"] ⟶	
Income from continuing operations	xxx
[2] *DISCONTINUED OPERATIONS*	*xxx*
Income before extraordinary item and cumulative effect of accounting change	xxx
[3] *EXTRAORDINARY ITEM*	*xxx*
[4] *CUMULATIVE EFFECT ON PRIOR YEARS OF CHANGE IN ACCOUNTING PRINCIPLE*	*xxx*
Net income	$xxx

SPECIAL OR UNUSUAL ITEMS

GAAPrequire that special or unusual items be reported as a component of income from continuing operations, but management may also want to break them out to indicate their unusual nature so that analysts and others may decide that these items will not affect future operations and exclude them from computations of core earnings.

Some items that may qualify as special or unusual:

- Inventory write-downs.
- Gains or losses caused by foreign exchange fluctuations.
- Restructuring charges.
- Write-downs of receivables.
- Contract price adjustments.
- Gains or losses from asset sales.
- Losses due to a strike, including those against competitors or major suppliers.[1]

Because there are a number of gray areas in classifying items, it is possible to engage in earnings management when making decisions about where items should fall. For example, disposition of a major manufacturing plant could be classified in either (1) Special or Unusual Charges or (2) Discontinued Operations. The correct classification may depend on executive judgment about factors like those discussed in the detailed GAAP requirements for reporting items as Discontinued Operations.

CASE STUDY: LEVI STRAUSS—UNUSUAL LOSS[2]

As you can see from the bolded item in Figure 17.2, the income statement for fiscal year ended November 26, 2000, the well-known clothing company Levi Strauss had a special or unusual loss item, Excess Capacity Reduction/Restructuring in the amount of $33,144,000. Management chose to break out this item in reporting regular operating income. Though only about 15 percent of net income after tax, the loss was apparently significant enough that management did not want to bury it in other expenses. (The item would have been approximately 10 percent of net income after tax if reported on a net-of-tax basis but GAAP does not permit this.)

---

[1] APB 30: Reporting the Results of Operations—Reporting the Effects of Disposal of a Segment of a Business, and Extraordinary, Unusual and Infrequently Occurring Events and Transactions. *http://www.pwccomperio.com/search97cgi/s97is_english.dll/ search97cgi/inetsrch_english.ini?action=formgen&Template=comperio.hts.* Accessed December 18, 2001.

[2] Levi Strauss 10-K for Fiscal Year Ending November 26, 2000. *http://www.sec.gov/ Archives/edgar/data/94845/000009484501000015/0000094845-01-000015-0001.txt.* Accessed December 17, 2001.

Figure 17.2. Levi Strauss Income Statement

```
          LEVI STRAUSS & CO. AND SUBSIDIARIES
            CONSOLIDATED STATEMENTS OF INCOME
        (DOLLARS IN THOUSANDS, EXCEPT PER SHARE DATA)

                                          YEAR ENDED
                                       NOVEMBER 26, 2000
Net sales . . . . . . . . . . . . . . . . . . $4,645,126
Cost of goods sold . . . . . . . . . . . . . . 2,690,170
Gross profit . . . . . . . . . . . . . . . . . 1,954,956

Marketing, general and administrative expenses 1,481,718
Other operating income . . . . . . . . . . . . (32,380)
```
Excess capacity reduction/restructuring. . . . (33,144)
```
Operating income. . . . . . . . . . . . . . . . 538,762

Interest expense. . . . . . . . . . . . . . . . 234,098
Other (income) expense, net . . . . . . . . . . (39,016)
Income before taxes . . . . . . . . . . . . . . 343,680
Provision for taxes. . . . . . . . . . . . . . . 120,288

Net income . . . . . . . . . . . . . . . . . . $223,392
```
(emphasis added)

DISCONTINUED OPERATIONS

As we discussed in the big bath chapter, for a business to shed some of its operations and qualify them as discontinued, the operations and cash flows to be disposed of must be a clearly distinguishable component of the business—physically and operationally separable from other activities of the company. Any of the following may qualify as such a component:

- Reportable segment (defined in FASB 131).
- Operating segment (defined in FASB 131).
- Reporting unit (defined in FASB 142).
- Asset group (defined in FASB 144).

Since discontinued operations, by definition, will not exist in the future, they should not be included in estimates of core earnings. Executives will therefore prefer that operations they dispose of qualify for discontinued operations treatment if that is within GAAP.

EXTRAORDINARY ITEMS

GAAP defines as extraordinary items any nonrecurring material gains or losses that have both the following characteristics:

- *Unusual in nature* due to abnormal events that are not directly related to the typical operations of the business.
- *Infrequent in their occurrence.* The result of an event that is not reasonably expected to recur for the business.

Extraordinary gains or losses must be presented, net of any tax effects, below the line, after operating income.

Since extraordinary items are by definition infrequent, they are not to be included in estimates of core earnings. Management will report items as extraordinary, to the extent permitted by GAAP if they do not want analysts to include their effects in future earnings estimates.

Extraordinary gains or losses may be due to a major casualty. A $400 million loss suffered by a company that had operations in the New York World Trade Center on September 11, 2001, would clearly qualify as extraordinary.

Judgment is often required to determine what qualifies as an extraordinary item. Determining whether an event is "unusual" and "infrequent" may not be easy. Condemnation of a 100-acre tract of land worth $50,000,000 by a city government wanting to create a new park might qualify as extraordinary for the company owning the land, or it might not. The answer would depend on how often there have been previous condemnations and the expectation of future ones. If the condemnation created a large gain, the company might prefer that the item not be classified as extraordinary so it could be reported above the line in operating income. On the other hand, if it created a large loss, the company might prefer that the item be classified as extraordinary so it could be separately reported below the line, so that analysts might be willing to exclude the loss from core earnings.

EFFECT OF CHANGE IN ACCOUNTING PRINCIPLE

As discussed in the chapter on changing GAAP, most changes in accounting principle are reported by simply adopting the new method as of the first day of the current fiscal year so that the income statement reflect uses of the new method throughout the current fiscal year.

The effect of adopting the principle on years prior to the current fiscal year is shown as computed at the bottom of the current income statement, net of any tax effects, immediately before Net Income. To illustrate how the cumulative effect is computed, assume that at the beginning of the third year of its life, a company decides to change from straight-line to accelerated depreciation for a $1,500,000 machine that has a five-year estimated life and no salvage value. Table 17.1 compares the amounts of annual depreciation under the two methods.

Table 17.1. Annual Depreciation Comparison

Year	Straight-Line	Accelerated Depreciation [Sum-of-years digits]	Annual Difference Two Depreciation Methods	Cumulative Difference At End of Fiscal Year For Two Depreciation Methods
1	$300,000	$500,000	+$200,000	+$200,000
2	$300,000	$400,000	+$100,000	+$300,000
3	$300,000	$300,000	$0	+$300,000
4	$300,000	$200,000	-$100,000	+$200,000
5	$300,000	$100,000	-$200,000	$0
Total	$1,500,000	$1,500,000	$0	$0

As you can see from the accelerated depreciation column in the table, for Year 3, the year of the change in accounting methods, the company would record $300,000 of depreciation expense in its income statement. It would be reported under operating expenses, above the line.

The company would also have to record a cumulative effect that would reflect the effect on prior years as if the company had been using the new method all along. As you can see from the last column in the table, the before-tax cumulative difference in the two accounting methods before Year 3, the year of the accounting change, was $300,000. If we assume a company tax rate of 33 1/3 percent, the cumulative effect, net of tax, would be $200,000 ($300,000 difference - $100,000 of taxes). The company would have to record the $200,000 cumulative effect in a separate category at the bottom of the income statement below the line.

The earnings management effect of the change in accounting principles was that earnings in years 4 and 5 would have $300,000 less depreciation expense charged against them. Thus, management in effect increased earnings in years 4 and 5 by changing accounting principles in year 3.

CASE STUDY: CIRRUS LOGIC—CUMULATIVE EFFECT OF CHANGE IN ACCOUNTING PRINCIPLE[3]

The following information is taken from the fiscal year ending March 31, 2001, 10-K of Cirrus Logic, a leading supplier of high-performance analog and DSP chip solutions for Internet entertainment electronics, analog and magnetic markets.

---

[3] Cirrus Logic Inc. 10-K for Fiscal Year Ending March 31, 2001. *http://www.sec.gov/Archives/edgar/data/772406/000095013401503479/d88190e10-k.txt.* Accessed December 17, 2001.

During the year, the company had (1) a $14,362 ,000 unusual charge due to restructuring, (2) a $2,482,000 extraordinary gain, and (3) a $1,707,000 negative cumulative effect of a change in accounting principle. These items are bolded in Figure 17.3 so that they may be easily located. None of these three items was particularly large in relation to the net income of $143,176,000.

Figure 17.3. Cirrus Logic Reporting of Cumulative Effect of Change in GAAP

```
                    CIRRUS LOGIC, INC.
          CONSOLIDATED STATEMENTS OF OPERATIONS
         (IN THOUSANDS, EXCEPT PER SHARE AMOUNTS)
                                       FISCAL YEAR ENDED
                                       MARCH 31, 2001
Net sales . . . . . . . . . . . . . . . . . . . $778,673
Costs and expenses:
  Cost of sales . . . . . . . . . . . . . . . .  486,355
  Research and development . . . . . . . . . . . 127,599
  Selling, general and administrative. . . . . . 109,629
  Restructuring costs and other, net. . . . . . (14,362)
Total costs and expenses . . . . . . . . . . .  709,221
Income (loss) from operations. . . . . . . . .   69,452
Realized gain on the sale of marketable
  equity securities . . . . . . . . . . . . . .  86,886
Interest expense . . . . . . . . . . . . . . .  (11,759)
Interest income . . . . . . . . . . . . . . . .  18,168
Other income (expense) . . . . . . . . . . . .   (4,928)
Income (loss) before provision for income
  taxes . . . . . . . . . . . . . . . . . . .   157,819
Provision for income taxes . . . . . . . . . .   15,715
Minority interest in loss of eMicro . . . . . .    (297)
Income (loss) before extraordinary gain
  and accounting change . . . . . . . . . . .   142,401
Extraordinary gain, net of income
  taxes of $276 . . . . . . . . . . . . . . . .   2,482
Cumulative effect of change in
  accounting principle . . . . . . . . . . . .   (1,707)
Net income (loss) . . . . . . . . . . . . . .  $143,176
```
(emphasis added)

The company gave the following explanation in a footnote to its financial statements:

"*10. CONVERTIBLE SUBORDINATED NOTES*

During May 2000, we repurchased in the open market $28.1 million aggregate principal amount of our 6% Convertible Subordinated Notes. We recognized a $2.5

**million extraordinary gain, net of tax, as a result
of these repurchases.**

*In December 1999, the Securities and Exchange
Commission issued Staff
Accounting Bulletin No. 101 "Revenue Recognition in
Financial Statements." We recorded a* **cumulative effect
of a change in accounting principle in the first quarter of fiscal 2001 to reflect our adoption of new revenue recognition policies** *as a result of this guidance.
Effective with the first quarter of fiscal 2001, we
have recognized revenue on international shipments
based on customer receipt and title passage of inventory rather than on the date of shipment, which was our
historical method. The cumulative effect of the change
for prior years resulted in a charge to income of $1.7
million. The effect of the change for the fiscal year
2001 was to increase revenue $5.2 million, increase
cost of sales $3.5 million, increase income before
extraordinary gain and net income before the change in
accounting principle $1.7 million, and increase basic
and diluted earnings per share by $.02 per share.*

*During the first quarter of fiscal 2001, we also
changed our estimate of the amount of revenue that is
deferred on certain distributor transactions under
agreements with only limited rights of return. Results
for the fiscal period ended March 31, 2001 include
revenue of $5.4 million, cost of sales of $2.0 million and income of $3.4 million related to this
change in estimate." (emphasis added)*

18 EARLY RETIREMENT OF DEBT AND USE OF DERIVATIVES

This chapter discusses how to manage management by retiring debt early and by using derivatives.

Long-term corporate debts, such as bonds, are typically recorded at amortized book value. When this type of debt is retired early, the expenses incurred and cash payments required may be substantially different from book value, generating an accounting gain or loss. Executives can manage earnings when they select the fiscal period for early retirement of debt.

GAAP REQUIREMENTS

Debt is retired (also called *extinguished*) when a debtor pays the creditor and is legally released, either judicially or by the creditor, from any obligation for the debt.[1]

For most but not all debt, GAAP require that a gain or loss from early retirement be reported as an extraordinary item, at the bottom of the income statement even though it may not meet the normal criteria for such a classification. However, there are two exceptions to the general rule. The following debt retirements are *not* reported as extraordinary items:

---

[1] FAS 140: Accounting for Transfers and Servicing of Financial Assets and Extinguishments of Liabilities, a Replacement of FASB Statement 125. *http://www.pwccomperio.com/search97cgi/s97is_english.dll/search97cgi/inetsrch_ english.ini?action=formgen&Template=comperio.hts.* Accessed December 18, 2001.

- Gains or losses incurred on a retirement that results from a conversion agreement that is part of the original debt covenant.
- Gains or losses from cash purchases of debt made to satisfy current or future sinking fund requirements.[2]

Rather interestingly, GAAP also requires the reporting of an extraordinary gain or loss for early retirements accomplished by either debt-for-debt swaps (new bonds for old bonds) or debt-for-equity swaps (stock for outstanding bonds), and in both cases, no actual cash need be exchanged to trigger a reportable gain or loss. Debt-for-equity swaps occur both to smooth income and to "relax potentially binding sinking-fund constraints in the cheapest feasible manner."[3]

TRUST ARRANGEMENTS

Corporations have sometimes attempted to settle outstanding bond issues by placing in an irrevocable trust cash or securities sufficient to pay off the bonds at their maturity date. The trust holds these assets until the maturity date and then pays off the bondholders. This arrangement is sometimes called an "in-substance defeasance."

Under such an arrangement, though, the company is not legally released from the bond issue and thus is contingently liable if something should happen to the assets in the trust. For that reason, a trust arrangement is not considered as extinguishing debt and no gain or loss is recognized at the date the assets are placed in the irrevocable trust, as GAAP has made clear:

> *"This Statement requires that a liability be derecognized if and only if either (a) the debtor pays the creditor and is relieved of its obligation for the liability or (b) the debtor is legally released from being the primary obligor under the liability either judicially or by the creditor. Therefore, a liability is not considered extinguished by an in-substance defeasance."[4]*

CASE STUDY: QUANEX CORPORATION[5]

The following data is taken from the Quanex Corporation 10-K report for fiscal year ending October 31, 1999. Quanex operates primarily in three industry seg-

---

[2] Kieso, D. E., J. J. Weygandt, and T. D. Warfield. 2001. *Intermediate Accounting*, 10th ed. New York: John Wiley & Sons, Inc., p. 724.

[3] Hand, J. R. M. "Did Firms Undertake Debt-Equity Swaps for an Accounting Paper Profit or True Financial Gain?" *Accounting Review*, 64 (1989): 587-623.

[4] FAS 140: Accounting for Transfers and Servicing of Financial Assets and Extinguishments of Liabilities. A replacement of FASB Statement 125.
http://www.pwccomperio.com/search97cgi/s97is_english.dll/search97cgi/inetsrch_english.ini?action=formgen&Template=comperio.hts. Accessed December 18, 2001.

[5] *http://www.corporatewindow.com/annuals/nx99/page36.html.* Accessed December 31, 2001.

ments (1) manufacturing of engineered steel bars, (2) aluminum mill sheet products, and (3) engineered products. The income statement shown in Figure 18.1 shows that in repurchasing its bonds the company had an after-tax extraordinary gain of $415 thousand, as the footnote explains:

> *"5. Extraordinary Item*
>
> *During fiscal 1999, the Company accepted unsolicited block offers to buy back $9.7 million principal amount of the 6.88% Convertible Subordinated Debentures for $8.8 million in cash. An after tax extraordinary gain of $415 thousand was recorded on these transactions in the second fiscal quarter of 1999."*

Figure 18.1. Quanex Income Statement

Quanex Corporation
CONSOLIDATED STATEMENTS OF INCOME
Fiscal Year Ended October 31

(In thousands, except per share amounts)	1999
Net sales	$810,094
Costs and expenses:	
Cost of sales	639,911
Selling, general and administrative	53,104
Depreciation and amortization	45,322
Restructuring charge	–
Operating income	71,757
Other income (expense):	
Interest expense	(14,402)
Capitalized interest	1,611
Other, net	1,383
Income (loss) from continuing operations before income taxes and extraordinary gain	60,349
Income tax benefit (expense)	(21,048)
Income (loss) from continuing operations and before extraordinary gain	39,301
Income from discontinued operations, net of income taxes	–
Gain on sale of discontinued operations, net of income taxes	–
Income before extraordinary gain	39,301
Extraordinary gain on early extinguishment of debt, net of income taxes	**415**
Net income attributable to common stockholders	$39,716

(emphasis added)

CASE STUDY: SYNOPSYS INC.—EARLY EXTINGUISHMENT OF DEBT[6]

Synopsys, Inc. supplies electronic design automation solutions to the global electronics industry. Its products are used by designers of advanced integrated circuits, including system-on-a-chip ICs, and electronic systems. During its fiscal year ending September 30, 1998, Synopsys, Inc. recorded a $1.9 million extraordinary gain from early extinguishments of debt and a $26.5 million extraordinary gain from sale of a subsidiary. The two extraordinary gains were equal to approximately 45 percent of net income before extraordinary items. The gain from early extinguishments of debt by itself was only about 3 percent of net income before extraordinary items. This double earnings boost was well received by the stock market, as is shown in Figure 18.2.

Figure 18.2. Synopsys Share Price History[7]

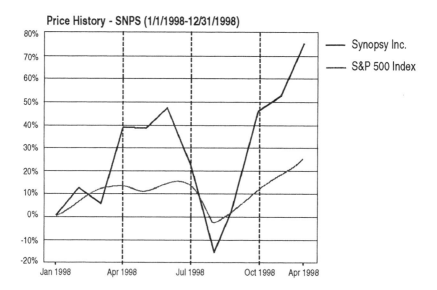

Price History - SNPS (1/1/1998-12/31/1998)

— Synopsy Inc.
— S&P 500 Index

---

[6] Synopsys, Inc. 10-K for Fiscal Year Ending September 30, 1998. *http://www.sec.gov/ Archives/edgar/data/883241/0000891618-98-005466.txt*. Accessed December 18, 2001.
[7] MSN Money. *http://moneycentral.msn.com/investor/charts/chartdl.asp?Symbol= snps&ShowChtBt=Refresh+Chart&DateRangeForm=1&PT=8&CP=1&C5=1&C6=1998 &C7=12&C8=1998&C9=2&ComparisonsForm=1&CB=1&CE=0&CompSyms= &DisplayForm=1&D9=1&D0=1&D4=1&D7=&D6=&D3=0*. Accessed December 18, 2001.

The following excerpt from the Synopsys 1998 10-K describes the nature of the extraordinary gains. The accounting effects are shown in Figure 18.3:

> **"Long-term debt.** *During fiscal 1996, the Company and International Business Machines Corporation (IBM) entered into a six-year Joint Development and License Agreement Concerning EDA Software and Related Intellectual Property (the IBM Agreement). In accordance with the IBM Agreement, the Company paid IBM $11.0 million in cash and issued $30.0 million in notes, which bear interest at 3%, and are payable to IBM upon the earlier of achievement of scheduled milestones or at maturity in fiscal 2006. The notes were recorded at fair value of $28.5 million, using a discount rate commensurate with the risks involved. The Company will also pay royalties on revenues from the sale of new products developed pursuant to the IBM Agreement. As a result of the transaction, the Company incurred an in-process research and development charge of $39.7 million in fiscal 1996. In the first quarter of fiscal 1998, the Company and IBM modified the terms of one of the notes which has been accounted for as an extinguishment of debt. Accordingly, the Company recorded an* **extraordinary gain of $1.9 million, net of income tax expense, related to the extinguishment of the note.** *As of September 30, 1998, the notes had a balance of $7.4 million, of which $3.2 million is included in long-term debt.*
>
> *During fiscal 1998, the Company sold VSI, the PCB/Systems design segment of the Viewlogic business to a management-led buy-out group for $51.9 million in cash. As a result of the transaction, the Company recorded an* **extraordinary gain of $26.5 million, net of income tax** *expense, in the fourth quarter of fiscal 1998. The Company retained a minority investment of 14.9% (fully diluted) in the new company."* (emphasis added)

USE OF DERIVATIVES

Derivatives are financial instruments or contracts whose value is either derived from (a) another asset, such as a stock, bond, or commodity, or (b) is related to a market-determined indicator, such as a stock market index. Derivatives can be used to protect against such business risks as:

- Interest rate changes.
- The weather.
- Foreign exchange changes.
- Commodity price changes.
- Oil price changes.

Figure 18.3. Synopsys Income Statements for 1998

```
                    SYNOPSYS, INC.
           CONSOLIDATED STATEMENTS OF INCOME
                    YEAR ENDED SEPTEMBER 30, 1998
              (in thousands, except per share data)
```

Revenue:	
Product	$430,979
Service	286,961
Total revenue	717,940
Cost of revenue:	
Product	36,371
Service	57,396
Total cost of revenue	93,767
Gross margin	624,173
Operating expenses:	
Research and development	154,407
Sales and marketing	245,376
General and administrative	47,179
Merger-related and other costs	51,009
In-process research and development other costs	33,069
Total operating expenses	531,040
Operating income	93,133
Other income, net	25,984
Income before provision for income taxes and extraordinary items	119,117
Provision for income taxes	55,819
Net income before extraordinary items	63,298
Extraordinary items - gains on Extinguishments of debt and sale of business unit, net of income tax expense	**28,404**
Net income	$91,702

(emphasis added)

Among the variants of derivatives are:

- Financial forwards (futures).
- Options.
- Swaps.[8]

---

[8] Kieso, et al., n. 2, p. 952.

The FASB concluded in 1998 that derivatives are assets and liabilities that should be reported at fair value. Gains and losses from derivative transactions are generally recognized immediately in regular income unless they are cash flow hedges, which are recorded in equity as part of comprehensive income.

Derivatives offer many opportunities to manage earnings. Suppose, for example, that a company had a large issue of bonds payable outstanding at a fixed interest rate. The company could enter into an interest rate swap that would effectively convert the fixed rate into variable rate bonds. If the interest rate increased, the company would then record an increase in interest expense for the bonds. Because the company chooses when to enter into a swap, it provides another opportunity to manage earnings.

CASE STUDY: EL PASO CORPORATION

During 2002, El Paso Corporation used derivatives to accelerate future profits from energy contracts into its current-year income. The $210 million of after tax-profits from the energy contract sales represented 55 percent of El Paso's total quarterly profit of $383 million. How did it do this?

El Paso owned a number of electric generating plants that had "long-term contracts to supply energy to utilities at well above current rates." Normally, the profit would have been recorded as El Paso supplied energy over the life of the contracts. However, the company "restructured" these old energy contracts into new contracts, one to supply electricity and one or more to buy it. Because the new contracts qualified as derivatives, they were recorded at fair value.[9] The bottom line was that "By morphing ordinary contracts into pieces of paper called derivatives, El Paso *front-loaded* all the profit it otherwise would have earned over a string of years."[10]

---

[9] Loomis, C. L. "El Paso's Murky Magic." *Fortune,* July 22, 2002, pp. 206-208.
[10] Ibid., p. 208.

19 "SHRINK THE SHIP"

This chapter discusses how a company can manage earnings by buying back its own shares.

Companies that repurchase their own shares do not have to report a gain or loss on their income statements because no income is recognized on the transaction. The reason is that, under GAAP, the company and its stockholders are considered to be one and the same. Income is earned only through equity transactions *outside the firm,* not with the firm's owners.

But if no gain or loss is reported on stock buybacks, what does that have to do with earnings management? The answer is that although a buyback does not affect earnings directly, it *does* affect earnings per share, a widely used earnings surrogate. That is why a stock buyback is sometimes a way for a company to manage earnings.

As we discussed in Chapter 2, a company that has 100,000 shares of stock outstanding and that earned net income of $300,000 in the current fiscal year would have reported EPS of $3.00. Management knows that net income is projected to remain at $300,000 for the next fiscal year, which will result in a flat EPS figure rather than the 10 percent rate that has been the market average for growth in earnings and EPS over the last decade. As shown in Table 2.1 (page 22), if the company buys back 9,100 shares at the beginning of the next fiscal year, it can raise EPS to $3.30 and meet the 10 percent average growth rate.

MANDATORY STOCK REPURCHASE

In many large companies, more shares are issued every year for reasons such as:

- Contributions to employee stock purchase plans.
- Executive stock options.
- Acquisitions of other companies.

This means that EPS will automatically decline unless shares are repurchased. In these situations it is almost mandatory that management buy back shares just to maintain the current EPS level.

CASE STUDY: NATIONAL SEMICONDUCTOR

National Semiconductor operates in the fast-growing markets for wireless handsets; information appliances; information infrastructure; and display, imaging and human interface technologies.[1] The company saw the number of its shares outstanding increase over several years for a number of reasons. For instance, in fiscal 2001 the company issued 3.2 million shares under a stock option plan and another 16.4 million shares issued in connection with a merger with Cyrix Company.

National Semiconductor therefore bought back stock during the 2001 fiscal year. As a result, total shares outstanding declined from 177,577,617 shares at the end of fiscal 2000 to 173,806,633 shares at the end of fiscal 2001 on May 27—an approximately 2 percent reduction in shares outstanding. This guaranteed an increase in EPS in future periods beyond what EPS would have been had the repurchase not taken place.

The per share data at the bottom of the income statement reveals that despite the share repurchases, the weighted average of common shares outstanding had nevertheless increased for two years in a row. This increase plus a large decline in net income meant that for the 2001 fiscal year actual EPS declined, but the weighted average will decrease once the entire 16 million share buyback program is completed (unless additional shares are issued in future years). To the balance sheet shown in Figure 19.1, National Semiconductor appended the following note:

> *"National has an employee stock purchase plan that authorizes the issuance of up to 24,950,000 shares of common stock in quarterly offerings to eligible employees at a price that is equal to 85 percent of the lower of the common stock's fair market value at the beginning or the end of a quarterly period.*

---

[1] National Semiconductor News Release dated January 25, 2001. *http://www.national. com/news/item/0%2C1735%2C598%2C00.html.* Accessed December 19, 2001.

Under all stock option plans, 3.2 million shares of common stock were issued during fiscal 2001.

In connection with the company's merger with Cyrix, 16.4 million shares of common stock were issued to the holders of Cyrix common stock. In addition, up to 2.7 million shares of common stock were reserved for issuance in the future upon exercise of Cyrix employee or director stock options or pursuant to Cyrix employee benefit plans and up to 2.6 million shares of common stock were reserved for issuance in the future upon conversion of Cyrix 5.5 percent convertible subordinated notes due June 1, 2001."[2] (emphasis added)

National Semiconductor issued the following news release explaining the motivation and scope of its stock repurchase plan:

News Release

January 25, 2001 - National Semiconductor Corporation (NYSE: NSM) today announced a second program of open market repurchases of up to 8 million shares of common stock. This program is in addition to a current authorization, previously announced on September 22, 2000, to purchase a similar 8 million shares. As of the end of the November quarter of fiscal year 2001, National had purchased 5.5 million shares under the first program. The timing of the purchase and the exact number of shares to be purchased will depend on market conditions.

"We are taking this action to offset dilution resulting from on-going stock-based employee benefit plans, as part of our commitment to delivering superior shareholder value," said Brian L. Halla, chairman, president and chief executive officer of National Semiconductor Corporation.[3] (emphasis added)

---

[2] National Semiconductor 10-K for Fiscal Year Ending May 27, 2001. *http://www.sec.gov/Archives/edgar/data/70530/000007053001500005/form10k_080101.txt.* Accessed December 19, 2001.

[3] News Release, n.1.

Figure 19.1. National Semiconductor Balance Sheets [4]

```
NATIONAL SEMICONDUCTOR CORPORATION
      CONSOLIDATED BALANCE SHEETS
    In Millions, Except Share Amounts
```

	May 27, 2001	May 28, 2000
Shareholders' equity:		
Common stock of $0.50 par value.		
Authorized 850,000,000 shares.		
Issued and outstanding		
173,806,633 in 2001 and		
177,561,617 in 2000	$86.9	$88.84

(Only the Shareholder's Equity section of the balance sheet is reproduced.)

```
   NATIONAL SEMICONDUCTOR CORPORATION
   CONSOLIDATED STATEMENTS OF OPERATIONS
```

Years Ended	May 27, 2001	May 28, 2000	May 30, 1999
	(In Millions, Except Per Share Amounts)		
Net sales	$2,112.6	$2,139.9	$1,956.8
Operating costs and expenses:			
Cost of sales	1,075.1	1,154.9	1,553.5
Research and development	435.6	386.1	471.3
Selling, general and administrative	328.5	312.3	317.4
Special items	51.9	(55.3)	700.9
Total operating costs and expenses	1,891.1	1,798.0	3,043.1
Operating income (loss)	221.5	341.9	(1,086.3)
Interest income (expense), net	52.0	15.3	(2.2)
Other income, net	33.6	285.3	3.1
Income (loss) before income taxes and extraordinary item	307.1	642.5	(1,085.4)
Income tax expense (benefit)	61.4	14.9	(75.5)
Income (loss) before extraordinary item	245.7	627.6	(1,009.9)
Extraordinary loss on early extinguishment of debt, net of taxes of $0.4 million	-	6.8	-
Net income (loss)	$ 245.7	$ 620.8	$(1,009.9)
Earnings (loss) per share:			
Income (loss) before extraordinary item:			
Basic	$1.40	$3.62	$(6.04)
Diluted	$1.30	$3.27	$(6.04)
Net income (loss):			
Basic	**$1.40**	**$3.58**	**$(6.04)**
Diluted	$1.30	$3.24	$(6.04)
Weighted-average common and potential common shares outstanding:			
Basic	175.9	173.6	167.1
Diluted	188.4	191.7	167.1

(emphasis added)

---

[4] National Semiconductor 10-K for Fiscal Year Ending May 27, 2001. *http://www.sec.gov/ Archives/edgar/data/70530/000007053001500005/form10k_080101.txt.* Accessed December 19, 2001.

CASE STUDY: INTEL[5]

Intel Corporation, the world's largest semiconductor chip maker, supplies the computing and communications industries with chips, boards, and systems building blocks that are integral to computers, servers, and networking and communications products. Between 1991 and 2000, net income increased from $819 million to $10,535 million. Diluted earnings per share almost exactly mirrored the income growth, increasing from $0.12 to $1.51 during the same period.

Intel has a stock option plan under which officers and employees are issued shares. The company also acquired other companies thorough the use of shares. The shares issued for these reasons were offset by a stock repurchase plan. Throughout the 1990s, the company repurchased approximately 1.4 billion shares a total cost of $22.2 billion. To see the effects of these transactions, see Table 19.1.

Table 19.1 Intel 10-year Financial Summary

(10 years ended December 30, 2000)
(In millions—except employees and per share amounts)

Year	Net Income	Diluted Earnings Per Share	Weighted Average Diluted Shares Outstanding
2000	$10,535	$1.51	6,986
1999	$7,314	$1.05	6,940
1998	$6,068	$0.86	7,035
1997	$6,945	$0.97	7,179
1996	$5,157	$0.73	7,101
1995	$3,566	$0.50	7,072
1994	$2,288	$0.33	6,992
1993	$2,295	$0.33	7,056
1992	$1,067	$0.16	6,872
1991	$819	$0.12	6,688

Share and per share amounts shown have been adjusted for stock splits through 2000.

The following statements were taken from the Intel 10-K for the fiscal year ending December 30, 2000:[6]

> "Common stock
> **Stock repurchase program** The company has an ongoing authorization, as amended, from the Board of Directors to repurchase up to 1.5 billion shares of Intel's common stock in open market or negotiated transac-

---

[5] Intel Corp. 10-K for Fiscal Year Ending December 30, 2000. *http://www.sec.gov/ Archives/edgar/data/50863/000091205701503434/a2040883zex-13.htm.* Accessed December 19, 2001.
[6] Ibid.

tions. During 2000, the company repurchased 73.5 mil-
lion shares of common stock at a cost of $4.0 bil-
lion. As of December 30, 2000, the company had **repur-**
chased and retired approximately 1.4 billion shares at
a cost of $22.2 billion since the program began in
1990. *As of December 30, 2000, 126.7 million shares*
remained available under the repurchase authoriza-
tion. " (emphasis added)

The data in Table 19.1 are illustrated in Figure 19.2, which demonstrates clearly that while shares outstanding is an almost flat line, net income and EPS have increased almost in tandem.

Figure 19.2. Intel Shares Outstanding in Relation to Earnings

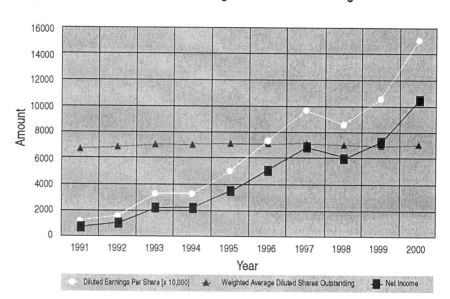

It appears that Intel has not tried to increase EPS by buying back shares but rather has used the buyback program to try to maintain a relatively constant number of shares outstanding. Of course, if the company had not employed the buyback program the increase in EPS over the last decade would have been much less dramatic.

EPILOGUE

Recent media revelations of financial reporting shenanigans or even fraud committed by a wide variety of publicly held companies has been a lightning rod for intense political scrutiny. The alleged frauds at Enron and WorldCom were so large and alarmed the capital markets to such an extent that both Congress and the President became concerned about insuring that corporate earnings were properly reported. The result was the Sarbanes-Oxley Act of 2002, which was intended to restore investor confidence in the capital markets.

Earnings management, as defined in this book, is not the same as fraud.

Since earnings affect the financial well-being of every company, the management, as well as the generation of earnings, is a legitimate area for corporate executives to focus on. Research evidence clearly shows that legal earnings management is widespread.

We can all think of things that we at one time were thought to be bad which later, with more research, turned out not to be. For instance:

> *"Medical research revealed that cholesterol is not just an artery-hardening villain; it serves a complex and essential physiological function in our bodies. Similarly, accounting research shows that income manipulation is not an unmitigated evil; with limits, it promotes efficiency."*[1]

GAAP offers many alternative accounting treatments and options. A smart manager will use the earnings management principles discussed in this book to stay within GAAP while presenting the best possible financial picture for the company since *the financial reporting system permits and encourages earnings management.*

This book will allow you to both understand and appropriately manage earnings.

---

[1] Arya, A., J. C. Glover, and S. Sunder. "Are Unmanaged Earnings Always Better for Shareholders?" *Accounting Horizons,* Vol. 17 Supplement (2003): 111.

A EARNINGS MANAGEMENT EVALUATION CHECKLIST

This checklist can serve as a reminder of possible earnings management techniques.

Item	Earnings Management Technique	Chapter Coverage	Used? Yes	No
1.	Estimating sales return allowances.	9		
2.	Estimating bad debt expense.	9		
3.	Estimating inventory write-down.	9		
4.	Estimating warranty cost.	9		
5.	Estimating pension expense.	9		
6.	Pension plan termination.	9		
7.	Estimating percentage of completion for long-term contracts.	9		
8.	Restructuring operations.	10		
9.	Asset impairment write-down.	10		
10.	Troubled debt restructuring.	10		
11.	Discontinued operations.	10		
12.	Writing off in-process research and development.	11		
13.	Purchase of a subsidiary.	11		
14.	Timing of sale of securities for a gain.	12		
15.	Timing of sale of securities for a loss.	12		

Item	Earnings Management Technique	Chapter Coverage	Used? Yes	No
16.	Reclassifying securities in the investment portfolio.	12		
17.	Recording a loss due to impairment of an investment security Security Impairment.	12		
18.	Sale of a subsidiary.	13		
19.	Creating a qualifying special purpose entity and transferring assets to it.	13		
20.	Spinning off a subsidiary.	13		
21.	Volunteering for a new accounting standard.	14		
22.	Improving revenue recognition.	14		
23.	Improving expense recognition.	14		
24.	Changing an accounting estimate.	14		
25.	Selecting a write-off method for long-lived assets.	15		
26.	Selecting a write-off period for long-term assets.	15		
27.	Selecting a salvage value for long-term assets.	15		
28.	Changing a long-lived asset to nonoperating asset.	15		
29.	Selling a long-term asset.	16		
30.	Entering into a sale/leaseback.	16		
31.	Exchanging similar productive assets.	16		
32.	Reporting gain or loss as a special or unusual item.	17		
33.	Recording a gain or loss as an extraordinary item.	17		
34.	Retiring debt early.	18		
35.	Using derivatives to accelerate income or expense.	18		
36.	Repurchasing stock to increase earnings per share.	19		

INDEX